SOL

THE DESERT RAIDERS

SOLDIER G: SAS

THE DESERT RAIDERS

Shaun Clarke

First published in Great Britain 1994
22 Books, 3 Sheldon Way, Larkfield, Maidstone, Kent

Copyright © 1994 by 22 Books

The moral right of the author has been asserted

A CIP catalogue record for this book is available from the
British Library

ISBN 1 898125 08 2

10 9 8 7 6 5 4 3 2 1

Typeset by Hewer Text Composition Services, Edinburgh
Printed and bound in Great Britain by
Caledonian International Book Manufacturing Ltd, Glasgow

Prelude

'It's one helluva sight to behold,' Lieutenant Derek 'Dirk' Greaves said, shading his eyes with his hand. 'Very impressive indeed.'

The camp was located just outside Mersa Brega, in Libya's vast Cyrenaica Desert. It was a sprawling collection of tents, lean-tos, makeshift huts and caravans overflowing with the men of the 7th Armoured Division and Selby Force, 4th Indian Division, 6th Australian Division, Royal Electrical and Mechanical Engineers (REME), Royal Army Medical Corps (RAMC), sappers, a Cypriot labour battalion and the hundreds of ragged Italian 10th Army soldiers packed into POW cages near the southern perimeter. Though holding a vast array of artillery and tanks, the camp was also protected by British infantry divisions spread out in a defensive line consisting of a series of 'boxes' — slit trenches for the infantry, gun pits for the artillery —

surrounded by barbed wire and minefields, though these were far away, well spread out, and out of sight.

The camp itself, Greaves noticed, was ringed with the 25-pounders of the Royal Horse Artillery, an equal number of British six-pounders, Bofors anti-aircraft guns, stone sangars manned by teams equipped with Bren guns and 0.5-inch Browning machine-guns, and even some captured Italian 75mm and 79mm guns to be manned by infantrymen, signallers, orderlies and cooks if battle commenced. It also contained what appeared to be hundreds of armoured vehicles. All dispersed evenly behind the line, these included the M3 Stuart light tanks of the 8th King's Royal Irish Hussars, the Grant tanks of the Royal Gloucester Hussars, the Matildas of the 7th Royal Tank Regiment, the Bren carriers of the 9th Rifle Brigade, and Marmon Herrington armoured cars.

Beyond the perimeter, on all sides, Greaves saw nothing but the 'blue' – the soldiers' term for the desert – stretching away to the dust-wreathed horizon under a brilliant azure sky. By night the desert was freezing cold, but during the day the heat was fierce, shimmering up off the desert floor, hurting the eyes, making the sweat flow and leading to short tempers and fist fights. Tempers were also

2

sparked off by the constant dust, blowing every second of every day and night, covering everything, filling the throat and nostrils, getting into food and drink and even sleeping bags, and which swirled in moaning clouds and drifted over the plains of rocky ground, soft sand and gravel. The dust also charged the metal parts of vehicles with electricity, shorting out the engines, often stopping the vehicles altogether and giving the men electric shocks.

Even worse were the flies, thousands of them, all enormous, attacking eyes and ears, dropping into the tea and bully beef, the tinned 'M and V' (meat and vegetables), into the herrings and tomatoes and dehydrated potatoes, buzzing noisily, frantically, all day long, and making a visit to the 'thunderbox' to answer the call of nature a veritable endurance test.

As for the freezing nights, though there was some respite from the flies, an alternative torment came in the shape of lice, bugs and cockroaches and, if a soldier became too careless, poisonous scorpions. All of these drove the men crazy and led to frayed tempers.

Last but by no means least of their torments was a constant and hellish thirst. The water, which had to be transported laboriously from Cairo or Alexandria, was warm, salty, distilled sea water that just about kept them alive while failing dismally to assuage the unrelenting dryness of their throats. Foul to drink on its own, it was more satisfactory in a brew-up, though even then its high salt content curdled the tinned milk and filled the mugs with soft, disgusting curds. The tea was more refreshing than the water, but even that failed to quench their thirst.

In combination with the heat, dust, and insects, the thirst may have contributed to some of the men's crazier antics. Having just completed their spectacular rout of the Italian 10th Army, the Tommies were flush with victory and displayed it in the way they dressed. A company commander of the Argyll and Sutherland Highlanders wore an Italian brigadier's uniform with sea boots; British troops of the 2nd Armoured Division boasted Australian slouch hats, a *bersagliere's* plumed hat, or the regalia of Blackshirt colonels; soldiers of the 9th Australian Division bore captured Italian pistols, with binoculars slung rakishly around their necks, as well as wearing the ceremonial gold-braided tunics of Italian officers instead of their own plain army jackets. In general the men preferred Italian uniforms, usually obtained by bartering with the POWs, to their own.

This sartorial excess, Lieutenant Greaves had

noticed, was complemented by a great deal of high spirits, including the indiscriminate firing of enemy rifles and pistols, exploding Thermos bombs, a lot of showing off in captured enemy vehicles, collecting wild dogs as vicious pets, bartering with Italian prisoners, betting on organized scorpion fights, hunting gazelles and other desert animals. There was a surprising indifference on the part of most officers to such undisciplined, and often dangerous, activities.

Lieutenant Greaves, formerly with the Scots Guards, now 8 Commando, was there for only two days as an observation officer from the Middle East Headquarters (MEHQ) in Cairo and due to fly back the following day from Tobruk. Though he understood the men's high spirits, he did not approve of their behaviour. The scorpion fights, in particular, were a particularly vicious form of blood sport in which someone would dig out a circular shallow in the sand, pour petrol around the edge, set fire to it, then place two scorpions inside the ring of fire. The heat of the flames would drive the scorpions wild and they would viciously fight one another – so much so that often one of them would inadvertently sting itself fatally with its own tail. Another sport, equally unsavoury, was hunting desert gazelles, which the men would pursue in trucks, firing at the unfortunate creatures with their rifles. While the deaths of the animals had the undeniable merit of supplementing the men's rations, Greaves viewed it as yet another barbaric activity spawned by a combination of victorious excitement, post-victory boredom, and a general lack of discipline.

Since the start of the British offensive in December, these men, including the 4th Indian Division, had resolutely pushed back the Italian forces in Egypt, stopping their advance at Sidi Barrani, taking Sollum, capturing Bardia with 40,000 Italian prisoners, and then Tobruk, and finally, after two months of relentless fighting, cutting off the main body of the Italian Army at Beda Fomm, with approximately 130,000 enemy troops captured. Now, in the closing days of March 1941, aware that advance elements of General Irwin Rommel's Afrika Korps, including the 15th and 21st Panzer Divisions, had recently arrived in Tripoli and, supported by the Italian mechanized Ariete Division, were advancing across Cyrenaica, the men, still torn between high spirits and boredom, were in no mood for the necessary discipline of camp life.

Greaves would put this into his report when he returned to MEHQ, where the staff officers, known contemptuously as the 'gabardine swine' because their uniforms were made of that material and the Tommies thought they had an easy life, were anxiously biting their nails over the arrival in Tripoli of Rommel and his Afrika Korps.

Greaves could understand the Tommies' contempt for the staff officers back in Cairo. Life there was certainly much easier and, in some cases, even luxurious. And yet, while he was supposed to be going back on an RAF Hudson transport the following day, he realized he would prefer to stay in the desert. A man who thought of himself first and foremost as a soldier, not as an officer, he was experiencing the frustration of the born soldier with no war to fight.

Even as he stood there beside one of the Bofors anti-aircraft-gun sangars, contemplating the vast, seemingly empty plains of the desert in the dimming afternoon light, he saw a long, thin cloud building up where the blue sky met the earth on the eastern horizon.

'Looks like a sandstorm coming,' he said to Major Gervase Reynolds, 3rd Hussars, one of the Regiments of the 7th Armoured Division.

'I hope not,' Reynolds replied, tugging distractedly at his handlebar moustache. 'Bloody dreadful things. Make you feel you're being buried alive and bugger up everything. Absolutely the worst thing about this damned place, which has many bad things.'

'It certainly looks like a sandstorm,' Greaves said as he squinted into the heat haze, surveying the distant horizon beyond El Agheila. The cloud was taking shape as an elongated band of darkness that spread higher and ever wider as it advanced across the flat, sun-scorched plain.

'No wind,' Major Reynolds observed. 'Not the slightest breeze, Captain.'

Greaves sucked his forefinger and held it up. 'Damn it, you're right,' he said. 'No wind at all.' Continuing to stare across the dazzling plain, he saw the cloud growing and still advancing at what he estimated was about thirty miles an hour. Then a series of black dots appeared in the sky above the horizon, distorted in the heat haze, but growing fatter by the second, racing forward above the duststorm until, in under half a minute, they took shape as winged birds.

Greaves realized they were not birds when he heard a familiar, distant rumbling sound.

'JERRY!' someone suddenly bawled behind him.

As the distant rumbling grew louder, the silhouetted birds became a squadron of German Ju-87 Stuka dive-bombers, all heading straight for the camp.

'Damn it!' Reynolds exclaimed. 'He's right! We'd better take cover.'

Even as Greaves recognized the enemy aircraft and, like Reynolds, hurled himself down behind the stone wall of a 25-pounder emplacement, the air-raid sirens wailed and the men in the laagers roared instructions at one another, frantically preparing their Bofors anti-aircraft guns. Jeeps and Bren-gun carriers roared into life and raced this way and that, churning up clouds of sand, as some of the men, arriving late, raced after them to jump aboard or get hauled up by their mates. The many troops in the tents poured out to grab weapons and helmets, then rushed to find cover in the defensive trenches around the perimeter. Others burst out of the latrines, some still pulling up their trousers.

Greaves and Reynolds hurled themselves down behind the nearest sangar wall as the first of the Stukas reached the camp, primitive, ungainly and with swastikas clearly marked on their fins, and peeled off to begin their dive-bombing.

The Bofors gun in the sangar exploded into action with a deafening roar, jolting dramatically as it belched fire and smoke, forcing Greaves to cover his ears with his hands as sand and gravel whipped up by the backblast swept hissing across him. The other anti-aircraft guns began roaring at the same time from all around the perimeter as the Stukas, which had been growling softly in an almost slumberous manner, screeched loudly, making their first attacks, their machine-guns firing as they descended. The bombs exploded nearby with a catastrophic roar and Greaves felt the earth shake beneath him as some Stukas screeched directly overhead before climbing above the pall of smoke. A lot of Tommies opened up with their .303 rifles and Mark 6 Webley pistols, adding their staccato snapping to the general bedlam.

'Fat lot of good that'll do!' Greaves shouted to Reynolds, who was crouched beside him, removing his hands from his ears and shaking his head to remove the dust from his ears.

Reynolds glanced at the men firing rifles and pistols, then tweaked his walrus moustache and grinned. 'It'll do the men good. Make them feel less helpless. That's a good sign, old boy.'

The Stukas were slow in flight but extremely fast when diving, the pilots fearlessly holding their course, ignoring exploding flak and streamers, and not levelling out until they were practically scraping the ground, when they would release their bombs, wobbling visibly as the load was dropped. Then they would straighten up and ascend steeply, back through the black clouds of flak and criss-crossing tracers, gaining velocity even as the bombs were exploding around the British positions.

'Courageous buggers!' Major Reynolds bawled. 'Got to hand it to them, old boy. The Jerry pilots are admirable. I . . .'

He was cut short by a series of explosions that tore up the ground nearby, creating a mushroom of swirling soil, gravel and debris, including large rocks and sandbags from the wall of a nearby sangar. The screaming of an injured Tommy daggered through the general clamour but was swiftly blotted out by the even louder bellowing of the British six-pounders, Bren guns and 0.5-inch Browning machine-guns, and the captured Italian 75mm and 79mm guns. The gun positions were hurriedly being manned by infantrymen, signallers, orderlies and cooks, most of whom were stripped to the waist, gleaming with sweat, and were gradually being covered in a film of dust and sand as swirling smoke obscured them.

'The tanks!' Reynolds bawled, rising himself to his knees and jabbing his finger to the front.

Sitting up, Lieutenant Greaves saw the Mark III and Mark IV tanks of the Afrika Korps Panzer divisions emerging from a billowing cloud of dust, spread out over half a mile, followed by motorized infantry and six-wheeled armoured cars.

'God, there's a lot of them!' Greaves exclaimed.

'Too many,' Reynolds sighed. 'They must have broken through our defensive boxes, forming a wall between them and us, which means the boxes won't be able to help us now.' He turned away from Greaves and bawled for the nearest radio operator to come and join him. When a sand-smeared 4th Armoured Division corporal with a No 11 wireless set had crawled up to Reynolds, the latter grabbed the wireless mouthpiece, contacted the tank commander of the Royal Gloucester Hussars and told him to move out. Still holding the wireless mouthpiece, but with the switch turned off, he looked back to the front. 'Let us pray,' he whispered.

As falling shells exploded between the German tanks, the enemy's 55mm and 77mm guns opened fire, creating a curtain of smoke and fire. With the British guns responding in kind, the noise was truly hellish and made marginally worse when the Grants moved out between the gun pits and sangars, to engage the Germans on the open ground beyond the perimeter.

The Panzers emerged from their own smoke with pennants fluttering from wireless aerials and their treads churning up sand, gravel and billowing clouds of dust. Assuming hull-down positions, they blasted the Grants, which were advancing with their 37mm and 75mm main guns firing at once, creating another nightmarish curtain of fire-streaked, streaming smoke.

The battle was awesome, like the clash of dinosaurs, the tanks obscured in the swirling smoke and boiling sand resembling hunchbacked, fire-spitting beasts. But it was a battle in which the odds were distinctly against the British, who were greatly outnumbered and lacked the practised skills of the Germans. The advancing Grants were soon stopped in a gigantic convulsion of erupting soil, swirling smoke and raining gravel, many of them exploding internally, others losing their treads, the rest peppered by 55mm and 77mm fire, which also cut down the men trying to escape.

'Oh, my God,' Greaves said to Reynolds. 'It's a slaughter.'

Major Reynolds responded by switching on the wireless mouthpiece and ordering the Bren carriers to move out. As the Grants were exploding, bursting into flames, shuddering and belching oily black smoke, with the survivors clambering down from the turrets, some on fire and screaming dementedly, the Bren carriers moved out to give them cover. While the Bren guns roared, spraying the German tanks and the infantry moving up behind them, the

Tommies firing their .303s and M1 Thompson sub-machine-guns on the move from the open-topped armoured vehicles. Unfortunately, they too were slaughtered by the Panzers' guns, many falling right out of the carriers and slamming into the sand.

The British gun batteries then unleashed a heavy concentration that made the German Mark IIIs and Mark IVs withdraw slightly. But they did so only long enough to let their infantry move against the flank exposed by the advance of the British Bren carriers. Reynolds immediately called up the Northumberland Fusiliers, who soon arrived with their heavy guns and temporarily plugged the gap, allowing the survivors of the Bren carriers to make their way back inside the perimeter as darkness fell.

'Incoming message for you, Major,' the radio operator said. Reynolds listened to the earpiece, then handed it back to the corporal and turned to Greaves. 'We're pulling out, Lieutenant. Back to Tobruk. Let's get up and go.'

With the German tanks temporarily withdrawn, they were able to evacuate the camp under cover of darkness. Soon the tanks, Bren carriers, armoured cars, Bedford trucks, jeeps and marching men formed a vast column on the road leading back through the desert to the harbour town of Tobruk.

Unfortunately, with too many units on the move at the same time, there was an almost palpable sense of panic, with many men abandoning the all too frequently stalled trucks and running to get on others without bothering to check what was wrong with theirs. Other vehicles were abandoned when they ran short of petrol – even though there were many three-ton trucks loaded with petrol passing by on either side. This, too, was a sign of growing panic.

Eventually, however, without being fired on by the German big guns or dive-bombed by the Stukas, the men found themselves inside the perimeter of Tobruk, mingling with the Aussies, who directed them to numerous positions along the wired perimeter, between gun pits and slit trenches. The tanks and trucks were lined up behind the wire to afford further protection.

'You've got to hold that position at all costs,' Major Art Wheeler, 6th Australian Division, said to Reynolds. 'That's the order I've just received from the gabardine swine. Fat lot those bastards know!'

Spitting in the sand, Wheeler stomped off to supervise the activities of his men. Greaves and Reynolds did the same with their own men before taking cover behind their jeep. They had barely done so when German infantry broke through the wire a mere hundred yards away and surged forward through the moonlit darkness.

'JERRY!' someone yelled again.

A British lieutenant with a corporal and five troopers rushed out to meet the Germans, charging against heavy machine-gun fire. Two of the troopers went down, convulsing as the bullets struck them, but the others managed to reach the first of the advancing Germans, killing some with their bayonets before succumbing themselves to bayonet and bullet. The rest of the Germans then rushed through the gap, ghostlike in the smoke-filled darkness, followed by the tanks, which headed straight for the British gun positions, located three miles inside the perimeter.

About forty tanks managed to get through before the Tommies could bring up enough men to engage the enemy infantry and gunners who were trying to bring their guns through the gap. The Tommies shot up their crews before they could get into action and the Aussies, fierce fighters as always, did the same along the barbed-wire perimeter.

One German was trapped on the wire, bent belly-down over it, screaming in agony. 'Put that bastard out of his misery!' one of the Aussies shouted and another, not hesitating, rammed his bayonet down through the soldier's spine, slamming him deeper into the barbed wire so that he kicked convulsively before he was silenced for all time. The Aussie withdrew his bayonet with a jerk, then dropped to his knees, raised his rifle to his shoulder and started firing again at the advancing Germans, ignoring the bloody, twisted corpse on the wire beside him.

'Those Aussies are impressive,' Greaves said. 'I'm glad they're on our side.'

'Damn right,' Reynolds replied.

After the tanks went through, the gap was closed and no German guns or infantry got past the Tommies or Aussies.

'Let's get back to the defensive line,' Reynolds said. 'Leave the men to mop up here.'

While the medics raced out to the closed gap to tend to the dead and wounded, Greaves followed the major to his jeep, climbed in beside him, and was driven away from the perimeter, following the three-mile route taken by the Panzers. As the tanks could only travel at thirty miles per hour, the jeep soon caught up with them and Reynolds raced boldly between them, determined to reach the British defensive line before the Germans. He had just driven up over the crest of a low hill, giving a clear view of the British six- and 26-pounders, when the tanks behind him opened fire and one of the first shells came whining down to explode with a mighty roar.

Greaves heard the roar of the explosion, felt the blast hammering at him, then was picked up and spun in the air, before falling through a great silence. He smashed into the ground, bounced up and rolled over it, then blacked out.

Regaining consciousness, he found himself on a stretcher, being carried back through more explosions, geysering soil, sand and gravel, to where the big guns were belching fire and smoke. Laid down on the ground beside Reynolds, who was on a stretcher and covered in blood, Greaves, whose lower half was numb, was forced to watch the ongoing battle without being able to take part in it.

While he had been unconscious the Panzers had continued their advance, firing their 55mm and 75mm guns, with the tracers illuminating the darkness like neon lights. When the tanks were about 700 yards from the British gun positions, the gunners fired on them with their 25-pounders and anti-tank guns, about 100 rounds per gun, which temporarily stopped them again. Then the British tanks moved out to engage them and, with luck, push them back a second time.

Two of the heavy enemy tanks tried to get around

the British flank. One was hit by a 25-pounder shell and exploded, breaking down as it tried to struggle back. The other fired and hit the British 25-pounder and its crew, causing dreadful carnage before making its escape with the other tanks.

After knocking out seven of the Panzers with their 25-pounders, the gunners eventually turned them back for good. Escaping through the gap they had created when they broke into the perimeter, the German tanks left pursued by a hail of shells and bullets from the Tommies who had taken command of the gap.

A sudden, startling silence reigned until, as if only slowly realizing that they had won, the gun crews clapped and cheered.

Still stretched out on his stretcher and not able to move, Greaves felt a spasm of panic, then groping carefully, discovered that he had broken his left leg and badly bruised the other, but was otherwise not seriously hurt or permanently injured. Glancing sideways at Reynolds, he saw that although covered in blood, he seemed fairly perky.

'Are you OK?' he asked.

'Lots of blood from shrapnel wounds in the thigh,' Reynolds replied with a cheerful grin. 'Looks much worse than it is, old chap.'

'Well, we certainly appear to have given Jerry a

good hiding,' Greaves said, wanting to sound as cheerful as Reynolds looked.

'We did,' the major replied, 'but I wouldn't call it a victory. Tobruk is now surrounded by the Germans and in a state of siege. This could last for months.'

Greaves tried to sit up but passed out from the pain. He dreamt that he was relaxing on the deck of a ship with a cool breeze blowing across the open deck and cooling the sweat on his fevered brow.

Regaining consciousness a few hours later, he found himself lying on a stretcher on the open deck of a British destroyer heading from Tobruk to Alexandria. Glancing sideways, he saw Reynolds, now swathed in clean bandages and still relatively lively.

'Rommel,' Major Reynolds murmured as if continuing a conversation with himself. 'He's a formidable enemy.'

'We can beat him,' Greaves said quietly.

1

'I agree,' 24-year-old Lieutenant David Stirling said, packing his rucksack on his cluttered bed in the Scottish Military Hospital in Alexandria. 'Rommel's a brilliant general, a man to respect, but he *can* be beaten.'

'And doubtless you know how to do it,' Lieutenant Greaves replied sardonically, knowing that Stirling was a man who loved soldiering and was full of ideas. Born in Scotland of aristocratic lineage – his father was General Archibald Stirling of Keir – young Stirling was a bit of an adventurer, passionately fond of hunting, shooting and mountaineering, as well as being devoted to the Army.

'Of course,' Stirling replied with enthusiasm. 'I've been studying the subject for weeks. Saved me from going mad in this bloody place and kept the marbles ...' He pointed to his head

21

with his index finger. '... well polished. Know what I mean, Dirk?'

'Yes,' Greaves said, also packing his rucksack, for he, too, was finally leaving the hospital. 'If a man spends too much time in bed, his brain tends to rot.'

'Too right.'

Having been in hospital for over six weeks, Greaves understood the dangers of chronic boredom. He had managed to get through his own first few weeks by dwelling on how he came to be there, although it was rather like reliving a bad dream.

After being knocked unconscious by the explosion, he had regained his senses as he was carried on a stretcher through a series of explosions to the Regimental Aid Post a few hundred yards away. Placed on the ground in a large tent between men worse off than himself, including those classified as Dead On Arrival, he had to wait his turn while the harassed doctors and medics assessed the injuries of those being brought in, carried out emergency surgery, including amputations, and passed the casualties along the line.

Reaching Greaves and Reynolds, they found that the former had broken his left leg and the latter had suffered serious perforations of the stomach from shell fragments. Greaves's leg was put in a temporary splint, Reynolds's stomach was temporarily bandaged, then both were placed with other wounded men in an ambulance and driven to the Main Dressing Station in a white-painted stone building in an area being torn apart by the shells of enemy tanks and dive-bombing Stukas.

Lying on a real bed in a large, barn-like room converted into a makeshift hospital ward, receiving warm smiles from the RAMC nurses, Greaves nevertheless could not shut out what was going on around him: essential first-aid and medical treatment, including blood transfusions, the removal of shell splinters from bloody limbs, and even more complicated amputations and other operations. It was a grim sight, made worse by the moaning and screaming of men in terrible pain.

Greaves's broken leg was reset and encased in a proper plaster, then, even as Reynolds was being wheeled into the surgery for an operation, Greaves was picked off his bed, placed on a stretcher and carried out of the building, into another ambulance. He was then driven to the harbour of Tobruk where, under cover of darkness, he was casevacked – casualty evacuated – in a small boat to one of the four destroyers anchored in the harbour. Those swift vessels, he knew, were the lifeline to Tobruk, running the gauntlet of Stukas under cover of darkness to bring food, ammunition, letters, and reinforcements to the besieged harbour town, as well as shipping out the casualties.

While crates of supplies were being lowered on slings down one side of the destroyer, Greaves and the other wounded men were hoisted up the other and carried down on their stretchers to the sick bay located deep in the crowded, noisy hold. There they had remained until the ship reached Alexandria, when they were transferred from the ship to the present hospital. After a minor operation to fix his broken leg, Greaves had been transferred to the recuperation ward where he had been given a bed right beside his fellow lieutenant, David Stirling, who was recovering from a bad parachute drop.

The hospital was pleasant enough, surrounded by green lawns bordered by fig and palm trees where the men could breathe the fresh air while gazing at the white walls and bougainvillaea of Alexandria, as well as the blue Mediterranean stretching out beyond a harbour filled with Allied destroyers. Yet a hospital it remained, with all the boredom that entailed, and Greaves and Stirling had passed the time by swapping stories about their experiences, the former in Tobruk, the latter along the Cyrenaican coast, and speculating on the outcome of the war and how best it might be won.

Stirling was a man who liked conversation and was brimful of energy. Greaves liked him a lot.

'The problem with Rommel,' Stirling said, taking up a favourite theme, 'is not that he's invincible, but that we're going about him the wrong way.'

'Meaning?'

'Well, for instance, take those raids we made with Laycock along the coast of Cyrenaica. Bloody disasters, practically all of them! Why?'

Greaves thought he knew the answer. He and the energetic former Scots Guards officer had been members of 8 Commando, posted to General Wavell's Middle Eastern Army with other commandos on attachment to 'Layforce', the special unit formed by Colonel Robert Laycock to mount raids against the Axis forces in Rhodes, Crete, Syria, around Tobruk, and all along the coast of Cyrenaica. However, after a series of disasters which were blamed on a chronic shortage of manpower and equipment, Layforce was disbanded and the men and ships used for other, presumably more fruitful, missions.

'Bad weather,' Greaves began, echoing his own thoughts. 'Shortage of manpower and . . .'

'No! That's damned nonsense cooked up by MEHQ to save face. The raids were disasters because we took too many men, inserted by orthodox means – in other words, by sea – and so couldn't keep ourselves hidden; usually being observed well in advance of the raids by Axis reconnaissance planes. The Krauts or Eyeties on the ground were therefore waiting for us to arrive, all set to cut us to pieces and send what was left of us packing. The very idea of using up to 2000 men for raiding parties landing by boat is ridiculous. Impossible to keep such an op secret. Just begging for trouble.'

'We're back to your idea of hitting the enemy with small groups of men rather than whole regiments.' Greaves said, completing his packing, tightening the ropes of his rucksack, and glancing along the ward, his eyes settling on a pretty RAMC nurse, Frances Beamish, whom he hoped to get to know better once he was on convalescent leave in Cairo. 'It's become an obsession.'

Stirling laughed. 'What's a man without an obsession? How do you think I ended up in this hospital? By trying to prove a point! You don't use large groups of men, which are bound to attract attention. You use small groups of no more than four or five and insert them as invisibly as possible. If you land them well away from the target area, letting them hike the rest of the way, they can *really* take the enemy by surprise. That's the point I was trying to prove – and that's how I ended up in this damned hospital, wrapped up like an Egyptian mummy, as stiff as a board.'

Greaves had heard the story before. Learning that another former Layforce officer, Captain 'Jock' Lewes, Welsh Guards, had acquired fifty static-line parachutes offloaded in Alexandria, Egypt, for shipment to India, Stirling had charmed the taciturn but adventurous Welshman into joining him in experimental jumps with the chutes. Unfortunately, he and Lewes made two of the first jumps from a Valentia, an aircraft quite unsuitable for this purpose. To make matters worse, both men lacked the experience required for the task. After tying his static line to the legs of a passenger seat, because the Valentia did not have the proper overhead suspension for the static lines, Stirling jumped out the wrong way, snagged and tore his chute on the tailplane, dropped like a stone and practically crashed to the ground. He was lucky to be alive. In the event, he had been knocked unconscious by the fall and came to in the Scottish Military Hospital, badly bruised and with two damaged legs. Now, after weeks of treatment and exercise, he was, like Greaves, about to leave for a period of convalescence.

'Look,' he said, lifting a clipboard off his still

opened rucksack and waving it dramatically in the air, 'I even wrote some notes on the subject. Want to hear them?'

'I'm all ears.'

Stirling grinned. 'The Germans and Italians,' he read, 'are vulnerable to attacks on their transports, vehicle parks and aerodromes along the coast. However, plans to land the 200 men of a commando for such raids against a single target inevitably destroy the element of surprise when their ship has to be escorted along the coast – a high risk in itself for the Navy.'

'I agree with that,' Greaves interjected, recalling many of his own doomed ventures with 8 Commando along the coast around Tobruk, when the boats had been attacked by Stukas or Italian fighters.

Stirling nodded, then continued reading. 'On the other hand, landing five-man teams with the element of surprise could destroy about fifty aircraft on an airfield which a commando would have to fight like blazes to reach. Such a team could be inserted by parachute, submarine or even a disguised fishing boat. They would then approach the enemy by crossing the Great Sand Sea, south of the Jalo and Siwa oases, which Jerry doesn't have under surveillance. By making the approach

28

from that unwatched flank, moving overland under cover of darkness, the element of surprise would be total.'

'Makes sense to me,' Greaves said, 'except for one problem. The Great Sand Sea presents enormous difficulties of navigation and survival. I don't think we could cross it.'

Grinning like a schoolboy, Stirling held his forefinger up in the air, calling for silence. 'Ah, yes!' he exclaimed. 'But that problem's already solved. I've been hearing stories about a little-known unit called the Long Range Desert Group, composed mostly of old hands from Major Ralph Bagnold's desert expeditions of the 1920s and 30s. It's now being used as a reconnaissance and intelligence-gathering unit that operates in the desert with the aid of ten open-topped Chevrolet lorries. Those men know the desert like the back of their hands and could be used as a taxi service for us. We parachute in, make our raid against the enemy, then rendezvous with the LRDG at a preselected RV and get driven back to base by them. I think it would work.'

'Sounds fair enough,' Greaves said. 'The only problem remaining is to keep your newly formed group under your own command. I think it should be separate from the main body of the Army and devise its own methods of training.'

'I don't think the top brass would wear that,' Stirling said, placing the clipboard on top of the other gear in his rucksack and tightening the rope to close it up.

'Well,' Greaves said, smiling automatically when he saw Nurse Beamish coming along the ward towards him, 'tell them you want the raiding force to come under the Commander-in-Chief Middle East. In real terms that doesn't mean a damned thing – the raiding party would soon get conveniently lost in that command and you'd have virtual autonomy over your own men.' He grinned at Stirling. 'Naturally that presents you with another problem: how on earth do you persuade them to let you do it?'

'Oh, I think I can manage,' Stirling replied deadpan. 'I've already written a detailed memorandum on the subject for the attention of the Commander-in-Chief Middle East Forces. Once he's read it, I'm sure he'll agree.'

While recognizing Stirling's boldness, Greaves was struck by his naïvety. 'Are you joking?'

'No,' Stirling replied. 'Why would I joke about it?'

'If you submit that memo through normal channels, it will almost certainly get buried by a staff officer and never be seen again.'

'Which is why I'm going to deliver it personally,' Stirling said with a big, cocky grin.

Greaves was opening his mouth to reply when Nurse Beamish, petite, with black hair and green eyes, stopped between him and Stirling, smiling warmly at each in turn but giving most of her attention to Greaves, who had flirted relentlessly with her during his stay here.

'So you two are ready to leave,' she said.

'Yes, dear,' answered Stirling.

'Corporal,' Nurse Beamish corrected him.

'Yes, dear Corporal,' Stirling replied.

'Where do you plan to stay in Cairo?' Nurse Beamish asked of Greaves.

'Shepheard's Hotel.'

'Oh, very nice!' the nurse said, raising her eyebrows. 'My own leave starts on Friday, but I'm restricted to a miserable leave camp. Perhaps I'll give you a call.'

'That would be delightful,' Greaves said. 'I look forward to it.'

Nurse Beamish smiled, nodded at Stirling, then turned away and walked off, her body very pleasantly emphasized by her tight-fitting uniform.

'I think you've made it there, old son,' Stirling said. 'That woman is keen.'

'I hope so,' Greaves said softly, and then, after

a pause: 'You're not *really* going to try delivering that memo personally to the C-in-C, are you?'

'Who dares wins,' Stirling said.

Lieutenant Greaves picked up both rucksacks from the beds, waved goodbye to the other patients, then followed Stirling. In an instant the Scotsman was on his crutches and out of the hospital to catch a taxi to the station for the train to Cairo.

2

While Stirling went off to the British Embassy to collect the key to his brother's rented flat in Cairo's Garden City quarter, where he would be staying, Greaves booked into the opulent Shepheard's Hotel, which was off-limits to other ranks and used mainly as a place where officers could meet their lady friends. Once booked in, Greaves shucked off his desert clothes, drank whisky while soaking in a hot bath, then shaved and put on his dress uniform. In fact, though Stirling did not know it, Greaves had a date that same evening with Nurse Beamish and would, when the time came, be wearing an immaculately tailored bush jacket and slacks. He was wearing his dress uniform for the sole purpose of escorting the cheeky Stirling to MEHQ in his bold attempt to take his memorandum personally to the Commander-in-Chief. While Greaves was of the opinion that Stirling did not stand a chance, he could not resist the opportunity of going along with him to see what transpired.

Dressed, Greaves drank another whisky by the window while looking out on the great sprawl of Cairo, with its bustling pavements, open-fronted cafés, shops, bazaars and its white walls strewn with red peppers and purple bougainvillaea, covered in green vines and shaded by palm trees. Here many of the women still wore black robes and kept most of their face covered; the men dressed in jellabas and sandals. Around tables in the cafés, some of which were directly below, the men drank coffee, smoked hashish pipes, played backgammon and talked noisily all day, ignoring the soldiers swarming up and down the pavements, hotly pursued by filthy, screaming bootblacks. It was a dreadfully noisy city, with radios blaring out shrill music and high-pitched singing, trams clattering to and fro, horse-drawn gharries clattering over loose stones, water gurgling from pipes and splashing onto the streets, and cars, including many military vehicles, roaring and honking in a never-ending traffic jam. It was also, as Greaves knew, a smelly city, but the closed window spared him that.

When he heard a knocking on the door, which was unlocked, he turned away from the window and told the visitor to enter. Stirling entered on crutches, his head almost scraping the top of the door frame. After kicking the door closed behind him, he crossed the room and sat on the edge of the bed, leaning the crutches against the bed beside him.

'I'll be glad to get rid of these things,' he said. 'What's that you're drinking?'

'Whisky.'

'Just the ticket,' Stirling said. While Greaves was pouring him a drink, Stirling glanced around the room. 'A nice hotel,' he said without irony.

'I think so,' Greaves replied.

'I notice it's conveniently located almost directly opposite Sharia il Berka,' Stirling continued, referring to the Berka quarter's notorious street of brothels.

'Quite so,' Greaves replied solemnly. 'That's where the other ranks are commonly to be found with a much lower class of lady than you'll find in this building.'

'Such as Nurse Beamish.'

Greaves grinned. 'Let us pray.' He handed Stirling the glass of whisky.

'Are you ready to leave?' Stirling asked.

'Yes.'

'Good. Let's go.' Stirling polished off the whisky in one gulp, handed the glass back to Greaves, picked up his crutches and awkwardly balanced himself between them.

'How much longer will you need those things?' Greaves asked.

'I can actually walk without them,' Stirling replied, 'but for short distances only. Then my legs start hurting. However, I should be finished with them in a week or so. Well, let's get at it.'

They left the room, took the lift down, crossed the lobby and went out of the hotel. Immediately, on the pavement outside, they were assailed by the bedlam of Cairo: blaring music, clattering backgammon pieces, the babble of conversation; the clanging and rattling of trams with conductors blowing their horns; and the roaring and honking of cars and military vehicles of all kinds, including the troop trucks of the Allied forces. To this deafening cacophony was added the growling and occasional screeching of the many aircraft flying overhead. They were also assailed by the city's many pungent aromas: sweat and piss, tobacco and hashish, petrol and the smoke from charcoal braziers and exhausts; roasting kebabs, *kuftas* and ears of corn; rich spices and flowers.

'The Land of the Four S's,' Greaves said, waving his hand to indicate the busy road and pavements, which were packed with Arabs in jellabas, women in black robes and veils, grimy, school-aged boot-blacks, and the troops of many nations, most of them swarming through the city in search of a good time. 'Sun, sand, sin and syphilis.'

'You can think about those while you take your pleasure,' Stirling replied. 'For now, let's stick to business.' He turned to the jellaba-clad hotel doorman and spoke one word to him: 'Taxi.'

'Yes, sir!' the doorman said in English, flashing his teeth and waving his hand frantically even before reaching the edge of the pavement.

Less than a minute later, Greaves and Stirling were sitting in the back of a sweltering taxi, heading for Middle East Headquarters.

As Greaves soon found out, even on crutches Stirling was both agile and adroit. When the taxi dropped them off at the main gates of MEHQ, he attempted to bluff his way in by pretending he had forgotten his papers and hoping that the sight of his crutches would dispel any doubts the guard might be harbouring. The ruse did not work, and although perfectly polite and sympathetic, the guard was adamant that Stirling could not enter without proper papers.

Unfazed, Stirling thanked the guard, turned away, manoeuvred himself on his crutches to one end of the long double gates, then glanced up and down the road, ostensibly looking for another taxi. But, as his nod indicated to Greaves, he had noticed that there was a gap between the end of the guardhouse and the beginning of the barbed-wire fence, and clearly he intended slipping through it when the guard was not looking.

His chance came within minutes, when the guard was leaning down, his back turned to Stirling and Greaves, to check the papers of some officers in a staff car. As soon as the guard turned away, leaning down towards the side window of the car, Stirling dropped his crutches, waved to Greaves, then led him through the gap.

'Act naturally,' he said to Greaves while gritting his teeth against the pain of his unsupported legs and trying to walk as normally as possible. 'Behave as if you belong here.'

Feeling an odd excitement, like a naughty school-boy, Greaves followed Stirling across the field to the main building of MEHQ. Just as Stirling reached it, one of the guards called out to him – either he had recognized him or seen his crutches in the road – ordering him to return to the main gate. With surprising alacrity, considering the state of his legs, Stirling ignored the guard and hurried up the steps to enter the main building, with an excited and amused Greaves right behind him.

Once inside, Stirling marched resolutely, if at times unsteadily, along the first corridor he saw, searching for the office of the C-in-C. Before he found it, however, he heard the guard behind him, asking in a loud voice if anyone had seen two 8 Commando officers enter the building.

Immediately, Stirling opened the first door he saw, which was marked 'Adjutant-General'. He came face to face with a startled Army major, who demanded to know what the hell he was doing bursting in unannounced. As Stirling was trying to explain who he was and what he wanted, the major, who turned out to be one of his old instructors from Pirbright, where Stirling had done his basic training, recognized him and became even angrier.

'Still acting the bloody fool, are you?' he climaxed after a lengthy tirade about Stirling's unorthodox behaviour, past and present. 'Well, not in this office, you don't. Get out of here instantly!'

Greaves backed out first, followed by Stirling, who was, to his amazement, grinning broadly.

'Worst instructor I ever had,' he said coolly. 'Come on, Dirk, let's keep searching.'

'I think we might be pushing our luck,' Greaves warned him.

'Tosh!' Stirling barked.

Wincing occasionally from the pain in his unsupported legs, he led Greaves further along the corridor, brushing past many senior staff officers, looking for the office of the C-in-C.

'That guard's bound to be trying to find us,' Greaves said, 'so if we don't come across the office of the C-in-C soon, he'll be on our backs.'

Stirling stopped at a door marked 'DCGS'. 'Beggars can't be choosers, Dirk. Let's try our luck in here.' Boldly, he pushed the door open and stepped inside.

Greaves followed him in and closed the door behind him. Though bold in war, Greaves now suffered a racing heart at the thought of facing the Deputy Chief of General Staff without an appointment, let alone a pass into the building. His heart thumped even more when he saw the DCGS, General Neil Ritchie, looking up in surprise from his cluttered desk.

'Who . . .?'

'Lieutenant Stirling, Scots Guards, sir,' Stirling interrupted breathlessly. 'And Lieutenant Greaves, also Scots Guards. Both with 8 Commando and formerly part of Layforce.'

Before the general could respond or get over his surprise, Stirling apologized for bursting into the office, explained that there had been no time to arrange it and said that he had come on a matter of particular urgency.

'It had better be,' General Ritchie replied darkly. Then, distracted by Stirling's ungainly stance, he asked, 'Why are you standing in such an odd way, Lieutenant?'

'Spot of bother with the legs, sir. Parachute drop. Just got out of the Scottish Military Hospital and had to leave my crutches at the gate when we sneaked into the camp.'

'You came here on crutches?' General Ritchie gazed at Stirling in disbelief, then smiled a little and leaned back in his chair. 'You have five minutes, Lieutenant. Take that chair and rest your legs. Then you'd better start talking.'

Relieved, Stirling withdrew his memorandum from the inside pocket of his tunic, handed it to Greaves, then gratefully sank into the soft chair facing the desk while Greaves handed the memo to the DCGS. Ritchie read it carefully, taking rather longer than five minutes, then spread it carefully on the desk and looked up again.

'Interesting.'

'Thank you, sir.'

'It could work, but I'm not at all sure that the C-in-C would welcome such an unorthodox approach. A sniff of guerrilla operations there, Stirling, and General Wavell doesn't approve of that business.'

'That may be true, sir, but rumour has it that he's under considerable pressure from Churchill to stop the relentless advance of Rommel.'

'Those rumours are based on fact. Nevertheless, he may not thank me for this kind of proposal. A lot of risk involved, yes?'

'It's a safe bet for you, sir,' Stirling said cleverly. 'If things go wrong, the casualties will be few in number. If successful, they could change the course of the war in the desert and bring credit to all of us.'

Ritchie thought about it, then nodded in agreement. 'All right, Lieutenant, I'll bring the subject up with the C-in-C. If he's interested I'll show him your memorandum. You should hear from me within a matter of days. In the meantime, no more nonsense from you – such as this break-in. I'll get a sentry to escort both you men out. Next time get a pass.'

'Yes, sir!' Stirling and Greaves said at once, with big, dopey grins.

The general picked up his phone and called for

a guard. Five minutes later a triumphant Stirling and Greaves were being escorted out of MEHQ. As they passed through the main gates, the guard who had pursued them stepped out, grinning broadly, to hand Stirling his crutches.

'Well done, sir,' the guard said with a grin.

Stirling smiled back at him, put the crutches under his armpits, and waited patiently beside Greaves while the latter hailed a passing taxi.

'Now we can only wait,' Stirling said, 'so let's have a good time.'

Three days later, when Greaves and Stirling were beginning to feel more exhausted from having a good time than they ever had on an operation, Stirling received a call from the DCGS's office, inviting him back to see General Ritchie.

While Stirling was at that meeting, Greaves enjoyed a long lunch with his attractive nurse, Frances, whom he had been wining, dining and bedding for the past two days and nights in his hotel. In fact, she had just left his room when Stirling turned up, flushed with excitement.

'The meeting wasn't just with General Ritchie,' he told Greaves. 'The C-in-C, General Auchinleck, was also there. So was the Chief of the General Staff.'

Greaves gave a low whistle of appreciation. 'So, what transpired?'

'Permission granted,' Stirling said, 'on the following conditions. 'I've just been promoted to captain. Five officers and sixty other ranks will be recruited. For the time being, we'll recruit only from former Layforce men. We'll train the men ourselves and prepare them for raids against five airfields Jerry is using as bases for his latest Me 109F fighters. Auchinleck felt that five-man teams are too awkward, so teams of four instead of five will be the operational basis of the raiding parties. Our parent body will be a non-existent Special Air Service Brigade, or L Detachment . . .'

'Why "L"?' Greaves interrupted.

Stirling's grin was mischievous. 'L for Learner. Anyway, that's what we're calling it: L Detachment, SAS Brigade. To Axis agents and others it should suggest that there are more than sixty-six parachutists in Egypt. Meanwhile, we can get on with the real business. Now let's go and find some men.'

Jubilant, they embarked on a search of Cairo to find the men who would be the bedrock of L Detachment.

The first officer, Lieutenant William 'Bill' Bollington, they found immediately, in the bar of

Shepheard's Hotel, where Bollington was staying. A Gordon Highlander whose father and grandfather had been senior NCOs, he was instantly excited by the idea of a new raiding team and agreed to join them.

'I strongly recommend Sergeant Ralph Lorrimer,' he told them. 'Dorset Regiment, but now with the LRDG. Apart from being a hell of an NCO in his own right, and an expert on the desert, he'd probably be your ticket to the LRDG. He's also, incidentally, unbeatable with the Browning 12-gauge autoloader. A good man in a tight spot.'

'Where will we find him?'

Lieutenant Bollington grinned and pointed down through his room window, in the direction of the Sharia il Berka. 'Down there. He practically lives in Tiger Lil's place. I think he keeps a room there.'

'Very good,' Stirling said. He and Greaves left the hotel and walked across to the notorious street of brothels. Tiger Lil's was a gloomy, echoing barn of a place where the men queued up at the doors of the rooms, often peeping through keyholes to see how the first man was getting on and shouting words of encouragement: 'Come on! Get on with it! We're all waiting out here!' Tiger Lil, the immense, good-natured madam, who was sitting behind the cash desk by the front door, told them the number of Lorrimer's room. As they climbed the stairs, they came across many young girls, no more than eight or nine, who were running in and out of the rooms with towels, cleaning rags and bottles of Condy's disinfectant.

When Stirling and Greaves reached the room which was, according to Tiger Lil, rented permanently by Lorrimer, Greaves hammered on the door with his fist and a gravelly male voice bid him enter. Doing so, he and Stirling found Sergeant Lorrimer, wearing his shirt and trousers, though bare-footed, stretched out on his bed, propped up slightly with pillows, reading the latest edition of *The Strand*.

Surprised to see two officers in his room, he slid his feet down to the floor and sat on the edge of his bed. He was of medium height, but broad-chested and muscular, with a handsome, world-weary face and a fearless, blue-eyed gaze.

'Yes, sirs?' he asked, clearly puzzled by their presence in his room.

Stirling introduced himself and Greaves, then explained why they had come. As soon as he had finished, Lorrimer agreed to join up.

'Can you get us the cooperation of the LRDG?' Stirling asked.

'Yes, I think so.'

46

'Excellent. Please get in touch with them immediately, then contact me here.' He scribbled his brother's private phone number on a piece of paper and gave it to Lorrimer. 'That's where I'm staying while I'm in Cairo. Get in touch when you've fixed up a meeting with the LRDG. If it can't be arranged immediately, fix it up for later.' He was leaving the room with Greaves when the latter, unable to contain his curiosity, turned back and asked Lorrimer: 'Do you rent this room on a full-time basis, Sergeant?'

Lorrimer nodded. 'Only during my leave periods,' he said. 'I'm a married man with three kids and a healthy sexual appetite. This room's cheaper than anything else I could hire and the girls are conveniently located. What more could a man want?'

'You're a man of initiative,' Greaves replied. 'I think we made the right choice. See you soon, Sergeant.'

Their next stop was the MP barracks at Bab el Hadid, where one of Greaves's favourite men, Captain Patrick 'Paddy' Callaghan, No 3 Commando, was languishing in one of the cells, pending a court martial for knocking out his commanding officer. Formerly an Irish rugby international and accomplished boxer, Callaghan was normally an amiable, courteous man, but unfortunately he had a violent temper. Indeed, before actually striking his commanding officer, Callaghan had run him out of the officers' mess at the point of a bayonet. He was, nevertheless, an exceptional soldier who had already been mentioned in dispatches for his bravery in action.

When Stirling and Greaves proposed that he avoid his pending court martial by joining their new unit, he said, 'Why not? I'm going out of my mind with boredom here. Count me in, gentlemen.'

The rest of the main group had to be searched out across the length and breadth of Cairo, in nightclubs such as Groppi's, the Blue Nile and the Sweet Melody Cabaret where soldiers, sailors and airmen, drunk on the deadly Zebeeb, groped the 'cherry brandy bints'; in the Union Jack pension with its egg 'n' chips and Greek proprietor; in the numerous bars and brothels of the Berka; in the healthier Springbok Recreational Club at Helwan; in the surprisingly sedate Cairo Club, which was a services club reserved for sergeants and warrant officers; and in the Anglo-Egyptian Union, an officers' club located outside the city.

From these and other places Stirling and Greaves, sometimes together, other times separately, trawled the rest of the men they personally knew, respected and wanted. These included Captain 'Jock' Lewes, Welsh Guards, former Layforce member, and the man who had made the first experimental static-line parachute jumps with Stirling. A superbly fit ex-Oxford rowing blue with a low boredom threshold, Lewes had already proven himself to be a superb exponent of night-time raids behind enemy lines in the Tobruk area. He also had a talent for devising training programmes and techniques, which Stirling intended putting to good use.

Finally, Stirling called for general volunteers, inviting them to a meeting in a tent in Geneifa, outside Cairo. Among those who came forward were Sergeants Bob Tappman, Pat Riley and Ernie Bond; Corporals Jim Almonds, 'Benny' Bennett, Jack 'Taff' Clayton and Reg Seekings; and Privates Neil Moffatt, Frank 'Frankie' Turner and Jimmy 'Jimbo' Ashman.

A few days later these men and more were gathered together at the chosen base camp at Kabrit, in the Suez Canal zone, to begin their special, brutal training.

They were called the 'Originals'.

3

Located by the Great Bitter Lake, about 95 miles east of Cairo, and south of Aden, Kabrit was a desolate piece of flatland, fully exposed to the scorching sun, plagued by swarms of fat, black flies, and consisting of no more than three mouldering tents for the men, a command tent with a rickety card-table and stool, and one badly battered three-ton lorry.

'Bloody hell!' Corporal Jack 'Taff' Clayton said as soon as he had jumped down off the back of the three-tonner and was standing in a cloud of dust with the others. 'There's nothing here, lads!'

'Not a damned thing,' Private Frank 'Frankie' Turner agreed, swatting the buzzing flies from his sweating face. 'No more than a piss-hole.'

The men were already wearing clothing more suitable to the desert: khaki shirt and shorts, regular Army boots with rolled-down socks, and a soft peaked cap instead of a helmet. Each man also had a Sykes-Fairburn commando knife and Browning 9mm handgun strapped to his waist.

'Damned flies!' Private Neil Moffatt complained.

'Bloody hot!' Corporal Jimmy 'Jimbo' Ashman exclaimed.

'All right, you men!' Sergeant Lorrimer bawled, his legs like tree-trunks in his floppy shorts, his hands on his broad hips. 'Stop moaning and groaning. Go and put your kit in those tents, then come back out here.'

'Yes, Sarge!' they all chimed.

Picking their kit off the desert floor, they crossed to the three tents and wandered around them in disbelief.

'These tents are in tatters,' Neil observed mournfully, wiping the sweat from his face and neck with a piece of cloth that could have come from one of the tattered tents.

'They're also too small,' Frankie Turner put in. 'Might as well sleep out in the open for all the good these'll do us.'

'More holes than a fancy Eyetie cheese,' Jimbo said, spitting on the ground between his feet. 'And how the hell we're all supposed to squeeze in there, I can't imagine. I think this calls for a talk with our soft-voiced friend, Sergeant Lorrimer.'

'Right,' Taff said. 'Let's pitch our gear temporarily in a tent, then we'll go and sort this out.' He ducked low to enter one of the tents and was immediately followed in by some of the others. The tents had been raised over the desert floor; there were no beds or groundsheets. 'Fucking beautiful!' Taff exclaimed. 'We're supposed to lie on the bloody sand and get eaten alive. Not me, mate.' Dropping his kit on the ground, he ducked low again and left the tent. The others did the same and gathered outside, where Lorrimer had indicated.

Lorrimer was over by the three-tonner, deep in conversation with Captains Stirling and Callaghan and Lieutenant Greaves. While the men waited for him to come over they had a 'smoko', which helped to keep the flies at bay.

'I can tell we're all going to be driven mad here,' Jimbo said, 'by these bloody flies and mosquitoes.'

'Creepy-crawlies as well,' Frankie said darkly.

'Snakes, scorpions, spiders, ticks, midges,' Neil said mournfully. 'You name it, we've got it here all right. We'll be eaten alive.'

'Dust,' Taff said, flicking ash from his cigarette and watching it fall to the desert floor, on all its hidden horrors. 'Sandstorms . . . Burning hot days, freezing nights . . . I feel ill already.'

'What are those two bastards talking about?' Frankie asked, gazing at Lorrimer and Stirling.

'We're about to find out,' Jimbo said, 'and I'm not sure I want to know.'

Eventually Stirling climbed up onto the back of the three-tonner and Lorrimer bawled that the men were to gather around. This they all did, most still smoking and puffing clouds of smoke.

'Sorry, lads, about the state of this place,' Stirling said, waving his right hand to indicate the tents behind the men, 'but I'm sure we can do something to improve on it.'

'With what?' Jimbo called out.

'Shut your mouth, soldier, and let the boss speak!' Lorrimer bawled.

'Boss?' Taff whispered to Frankie. 'Did he use the word 'boss'?'

'SILENCE!' Lorrimer roared.

'I appreciate your frustration, lads,' Stirling continued, 'but all is not lost. Indeed, I'm led to believe that there's a splendid Allied camp about fifteen miles south of here, where the New Zealanders, in particular, live rather well.'

'Is that some kind of message?' Neil asked.

Stirling's manner was deadpan. 'Without being too specific, let me merely remind you that your first priority is to complete the construction of this base camp by whatever means are at your disposal. I'll be returning to Cairo immediately to collect more vehicles from the Royal Corps of Transport and weapons from the armoury at Geneifa. When I get back here I expect to find things greatly improved. How you do it is not my concern; nor will I be here to witness it. I can only add the information that the Kiwis will be away from their base on manœuvres most of tonight and their tents will therefore be empty. That's all. Class dismissed.'

Taking the hint, a dozen of the men drove in the battered three-tonner that same evening to the large, fenced compound fifteen miles away, stretched out across a dusty plain above the Mediterranean and being used by British, Australian and Indian troops, as well as the Kiwis.

Deciding that the only thing to do was bluff it, Jimbo drove boldly through the main gate as if they belonged there. 'New Zealand Division!' Taff yelled as the lorry passed the bored Indian guard. Receiving no more than a nod of permission from the guard, Jimbo continued driving, passing row upon row of tents, tanks, other armoured vehicles and the many trucks of first the British, then the Indian lines, until arriving at the New Zealand area. There he switched off the headlights and the rest of the men piled out, letting their eyes adjust to the darkness, then using torches to locate what they needed in the tents temporarily vacated by the Kiwis.

It took them quite a while, but it was well worth the effort, for they managed to pile the three-tonner high with lamps, tables, chairs, steel lockers, wash-basins, mirrors, cooking utensils, proper camp beds, mattresses, sheets, towels, portable showers and latrines, tents large and small, camouflage netting, and even crates of beer and spirits.

'Come on, lads!' Taff whispered when they had been busily thieving for an hour. 'Let's take this lot back to base. Then we'll return for some more.'

'You've got a fucking nerve,' Jimbo said, grinning.

'Piece of piss,' Taff replied.

They made three runs in all, boldly driving in and out of the camp, waving cheerily at the Indian guard and passing the British and Indian lines as if they belonged there. Eventually, even the daring Taff checked his watch, noted that it was almost dawn, and became a bit nervous.

'Let's pack it in and get out of here,' he told them. 'It'll soon be first light and the Kiwis will probably return then. We can't afford to get caught now.'

'Right,' Frankie agreed. 'Let's get going.'

They were hurrying out of the last, largest tent,

obviously used as a mess tent, when the musically inclined Jimbo stopped, stared lovingly at a dust-covered item in one corner, near a long trestle table, and said, 'Oh, God, look at that beauty!'

'What?' Neil asked, perplexed.

'I want her. I *need* her!'

The rest stared at Jimbo as if he was mad. 'Are you kidding?' Frankie asked eventually. 'That's a bloody *piano!*'

Jimbo ran his fingers lovingly over the keyboard without making any sound. 'A real darlin', lads. Going to waste here. It could cheer things up a bit in our mess – *when* we get a mess going. What about it?'

'Jesus, Jimbo!'

'We could have a regular Saturday night. Make the beer slip down even smoother. Come on, lads, let's grab it.'

'Oh, for fuck's sake,' Taff said, exasperated and amused at the same time. 'Just grab the bloody thing and let's go. Move it, lads! *Now!*'

The piano was humped onto the lorry, easily placed there because this last load was light, then the dozen men climbed up to seat themselves around it. Jimbo then drove boldly back through the camp and waved as usual to the Indian guard at the main gate. The latter, seeing the piano, looked suspicious for the first time, but Jimbo was off and gone in a cloud of dust before he could be stopped.

Once back at Kabrit, where the sun was shedding dawn light over the Great Bitter Lake, painting it crimson, the men unloaded their last haul, had a brew-up and cold breakfast to get them through to lunchtime. They then enthusiastically raised the brand-new tents they had stolen, camouflaged them with the netting, filled them with beds, steel lockers, tables and chairs, hung mirrors from the uprights, filled the lockers with their belongings, and placed family photos on their tables and cupboards.

When their sleeping arrangements had been sorted out, they raised the biggest tent, to be used as the mess tent, helped the cook set up his kitchen, carried in the long trestle tables and chairs, stacked the crates of beer and spirits beside a refrigerator run off a portable electric generator, and finally wheeled the piano in.

Jimbo stood back to admire it. 'Looks beautiful, don't it?'

'A real treat,' Frankie told him. 'What about a tune?'

'You mean now?'

'Why not? Having just nicked it, we'd like

to know if you can actually play the fucking thing.'

'I can play,' Jimbo said.

When he had expertly given them a Vera Lynn medley, his fingers light on the keys, they all gathered outside to help two former REME men raise the portable showers and thunderboxes. Jimbo had an experimental shit and pronounced the latrines operational. For the rest of the hour leading up to lunchtime, there was a general rush to make use of them.

Later that day Stirling returned from Cairo in a jeep, leading a convoy of other jeeps and lorries for the use of L Detachment. When the vehicles had been parked, the Royal Corps of Transport drivers climbed into a Bedford and were driven back to their own base at Geneifa. Stirling then told his SAS troopers to unload the assortment of large and small weapons he had brought in one of the lorries. These included the brand-new Sten gun, Vickers and Browning heavy machine-guns, the M1 Thompson sub-machine-gun, and the obligatory Bren light machine-gun. These were stacked up in one of the smaller tents, to be used as an armoury under the charge of Corporal Jim Almonds.

By nightfall, when the burning heat was being replaced by freezing cold, the desolate 'piss-hole'

of Kabrit was a well-equipped operational base
and Jimbo was playing the piano in the noisy
mess tent.

4

Their training began at first light the next day with a more intensive weapons course than any of them had ever undergone before. Assuming that their greatest need would be for a barrage of fire at relatively close range to cover a hasty retreat after acts of sabotage, Sergeant Lorrimer gave only cursory attention to the standard bolt-action rifles and instead concentrated on the new 9mm Sten sub-machine-gun. This was only 762mm long, weighed a mere 3.70kg, was cheap and crude in construction, with a simple metal stock and short barrel, yet could fire 550 rounds per minute from 32-round box magazines and had an effective range of 45 yards.

To cover the same needs, great attention was also given to the M1 Thompson sub-machine-gun, better known as the 'tommy-gun' and immortalized by the Hollywood gangster movies of the 1930s and early 40s. A heavier, more accurate and powerful weapon, the tommy-gun had a solid wooden stock and grip, a longer barrel, and could fire 11.43 rounds at the rate of 700 per minute from 30-round box magazines, with an effective range of 60 yards.

Everyone was also retrained in the use of the 0.5-inch Browning heavy machine-gun, which could fire 400–500 rounds per minute from a belt feed, and was effective up to 1600 yards; the beloved Bren gun, the finest light machine-gun in existence, which could fire 520 rounds per minute from 30-round box magazines and was effective up to 650 yards; and finally the lethal Vickers 'K' .303-inch machine-gun, actually an aircraft weapon, which fired 500 rounds per minute from 100-round magazines filled with a mixture of tracer, armour-piercing incendiary and ball bullets.

This stage of the training was undertaken on a primitive firing range that was really no more than a flat stretch of desert, baked by a fierce sun, often covered in wind-blown dust, forever filled with buzzing flies and whining mosquitoes, and with crudely painted targets raised on wooden stakes at the far end, overlooking the glittering Great Bitter Lake. The firing range was also used for training in the use of 500g and 1kg hand-grenades, including the pineapple-shaped '36' grenade and captured German 'potato mashers', which had a screw-on canister at one end, a screw cap at the other and a wooden handle.

'These Kraut grenades are better than ours,' Frankie observed, 'because this nice long wooden handle makes them easier to throw.'

In fact, most of the men, once over their initial nervousness, enjoyed throwing all kind of grenades and watching the great mushrooms of sand, soil and gravel boiling up from the desert floor with a deafening roar. It made them feel powerful.

'I can't imagine any fucker surviving *that*,' Jimbo said with satisfaction after a particularly good throw that had blown away a whole strip of the escarpment on which they were training.

'They *do* survive, Private,' Lorrimer corrected him. 'You'd be amazed at what those Krauts can survive, so don't get too cocky. You throw a grenade, think it's blown the target to hell, so stand up feeling good ... and you get your balls shot off by the Jerries you thought you'd killed. Take nothing for granted, lad.'

'Thanks for the encouragement, Sarge. I feel really good now.'

'NEXT!' Lorrimer bawled.

Training in demolition, which also took place on

the firing range, was given by Sergeant Derek Leak, former Royal Engineer sapper and ammunition technician with the Royal Army Ordnance Corps. A watchful, humourless man who had been burnt and scarred by the many accidents of his profession, he demanded their full attention when he taught them about low explosives, such as gunpowder, and high explosives, such as RDX or PETN, requiring initiators or time fuses and firing caps. Lessons were given not only in the handling of such explosives, but in precisely how they should be placed in a variety of circumstances, such as the blowing up of aircraft, bridges, roads or buildings, as well as the setting of booby-traps.

'I hate this shit,' Jimbo complained to his mates as he nervously connected a time fuse to a non-electric firing cap. 'It gives me the willies.'

'Yeah,' Frankie said sardonically, 'we can see that by the shaking of your hands.'

'This stuff is dangerous, lads,' Jimbo reminded them, trying to steady his hands. 'One mistake and it'll blow you to hell and back.'

'It isn't that bad,' Taff said, not handling it himself and therefore able to be more objective. 'It isn't really as dangerous as people think . . . *if* you handle it properly.'

'Is that so?' Neil asked morosely. 'Have you

noticed Leak's face? He's got more scars than fucking Frankenstein – and they all came from accidental explosions.'

'And *he's* a former sapper,' Jimbo said. 'An explosives specialist! So don't tell *me* it's safe.'

'For fuck's sake, Jimbo,' Taff exclaimed, suddenly nervous, 'keep those bleedin' hands steady! You almost dropped that bloody stuff then.'

Jimbo managed to insert the fuse into the firing cap, then sat back and smirked. 'Piece of piss,' he said. 'I believe you're the next to try this, Taff. I just hope *you've* got steady hands.'

As the training continued, with radio, first aid, nocturnal navigation, and enemy vehicle and aircraft recognition added to the growing list of skills to be learned by the men, it became apparent to them all that they were in a combat unit like no other, with no distinction in rank and everyone, including the officers, compelled to meet the same exacting standards.

The informality went beyond that. The word 'boss', first used, perhaps accidentally, by Sergeant Lorrimer, gradually replaced 'sir' and so-called 'Chinese parliaments', in which decisions were agreed between officers and other ranks after informal discussion, became commonplace. This in turn increased the mutual trust between the men and greatly enhanced the feasibility of the four-man patrol. Also, as each of the four men had a specialist skill – driver/mechanic, navigator, explosives and first aid – but all had been cross-trained to do the other men's jobs if required, this made them uniquely interdependent.

Their psychological bonding was made even solider by the harsh fact that anyone who failed at any point in the training, or who dropped out from fear, exhaustion, thirst or other causes, was RTU'd – Returned to Unit – without mercy. As the numbers were whittled down, those remaining were forming the kernel of an exceptional band of widely talented, closely knit and proud fighting men.

'We're the fucking *crème de la crème*,' Jimbo said. 'That's why we're still here, lads.'

The taciturn but brilliantly inventive Captain 'Jock' Lewes, who was constantly devising ways of testing the men to their limits, increased the chances of being RTU'd himself by introducing desert marches by day and by night. Not a man to demand of others what he could not do himself, Lewes turned himself into a guinea-pig by making the first marches entirely alone and gradually increasing the distance he had to hike, the length of time he had to go without water in the desert, and the weight he had to carry in his bergen backpack. Finally, he set himself precise navigation tests that had to be completed within a certain time.

'He's a fucking genius, that Lewes, I'm telling you,' Jimbo informed his mates. 'Remember that day he took me out on my own, just the two of us? He said we were gonna hike to an RV twenty miles away and that he'd know when we'd done exactly that. The desert's so empty – no landmarks to navigate by – I couldn't figure out how he would manage it. Then I noticed he was carrying lots of small stones in the pocket of his trousers and kept transferring them, one at a time, from that pocket to the other. When I asked what the fuck he was doing, he said he'd just devised this new way of navigating and measuring distance. What he did was count his paces. After each hundred steps, he'd transfer one of the stones to the other pocket. The average pace, he said, was thirty inches, so each stone represented approximately eighty-three yards. That way he could easily calculate just how far he had marched. Pretty damned clever, eh?'

'Too right!' Frankie said.

The men admired Jock Lewes not only for his many inventions and innovations, but because he never asked them to do anything particularly demanding or dangerous without first doing it himself. Indeed, regarding the murderous hikes into the desert, only when he had personally ascertained that they could actually be accomplished did he introduce them as part of a specific, extremely demanding selection course. These included nights sleeping in laying-up positions, or LUPs, scraped out of the freezing desert floor; signals training, covering Morse code, special codes and call-sign signals, all undertaken in the field; the operation of radios, recognition of radio 'black spots', and the setting up of standard and makeshift antennas; the weapons maintenance in the windswept, freezing desert darkness; the procedure for calling in artillery fire and air strikes; and general desert survival, both by day and by night. Those who failed to meet the rigorous standards set by Lewes were brutally RTU'd. But in view of the fact that Lewes did all those things himself, the men understood why.

'If he can do it,' Taff said, 'then we should be able to do it as well. If we can't, we don't deserve to be here. Lewes has set us the highest of standards.'

While Captain Stirling was forced to spend an increasing amount of time by himself, either developing the strategies to be used for forthcoming operations or commuting between Kabrit and Cairo to keep MEHQ informed of their progress,

Lieutenant Greaves and Captain Callaghan between them supervised the general training and ensured that the administrative side of the camp ran smoothly. They also, however, took part in the many arduous physical tests devised by Lewes and thus forged a close bond with the other ranks. This bond was further strengthened by the officers' willingness to forget their rank and meet the men on a level they understood.

For instance, one day, after Lieutenant Greaves had checked the men's water canteens to ensure that they had not drunk more water than permitted during their latest hike, a particularly troublesome trooper complained that the *officers'* canteens were never checked. Greaves instantly handed the man his own canteen and invited him to 'finish it off'. When the man opened the canteen, he found it completely full – because Greaves had deliberately made the whole hike without drinking a drop. This revelation, while shaming that one trooper into enduring his thirst, impressed all the other men.

Again, when the men were resting on a sun-scorched escarpment after another murderous march, Captain Callaghan, who had a short temper and took no nonsense from anyone, got fed up with a trooper complaining that they needed a rest. He grabbed the man by the shoulders, picked him bodily off the ground, and held him over the edge of the cliff, threatening to drop him into the sea if he did not shut his trap. The terrified man shut up and the other men, rather than resenting Callaghan, respected his flamboyant way of dealing with the situation.

When Captain Stirling heard stories like this, he felt even more guilty.

'I hate being away so often,' he explained to Greaves and Callaghan, 'but I simply have to keep pushing at MEHQ. Those sods don't approve of us – they think we're a bunch of cowboys – and a lot of them are actively working against us in the hope that we'll fail. I'd rather be here, working with you and the other men, but it just isn't possible. Please bear in mind, though, that if you think I need to set an example by taking part in a particular exercise, you have only to say so.'

'That's understood, boss,' Greaves said.

'I think the men understand the situation,' Callaghan added. 'As long as we officers do what *they* do, they'll be all right about it.'

Greaves grinned at that. 'And we do it, David, believe me. We have the bruises to prove it.'

Stirling nodded, relieved. 'I'll be with you when the raids commence,' he said. 'Of that you can rest assured.'

During one of Stirling's many trips to Cairo, Sergeant Lorrimer, as requested, fixed up a meeting between him and Lieutenants Beevor and Parkinson of the LRDG. The first meeting took place in the desert near Tobruk, where the LRDG was acting as a reconnaissance and intelligence-gathering unit under the very noses of the Germans. The two widely experienced lieutenants, both old hands from Bagnold's desert expeditions of the 1930s and now just back from another dangerous R and I mission around besieged Tobruk, were instinctively sceptical about the raiding-party concept of the immaculate, urbane Captain Stirling, but they agreed to read the report he had put together and give their response. The second meeting took place over glasses of whisky in the Anglo-Egyptian Union, the officers' club located just outside Cairo, where the same two LRDG officers admitted to being impressed with the report and agreed to act as a 'taxi' service to L Detachment when the first raids were mounted. The four men then shook hands and went their separate ways: Beevor and Parkinson back into the desert around Tobruk; a delighted Stirling and Lorrimer back to the sun-scorched camp at Kabrit, now more determined than ever to ensure that L Detachment became a viable entity.

Parachute training began a few weeks later with the building of a steel framework some 35 feet high, from which the men could be dropped to learn the skills of landing. While reasonably effective in teaching the men how to land properly, the static frames could not be used to simulate the vertical and lateral movement of a proper parachute drop. Stirling therefore contacted the only parachute school then extant, Ringway in England, and begged for assistance. Largely ignored, he asked the inventive Jock Lewes to devise their own methods of training.

After personally experimenting with various ways of rolling as his feet impacted with the ground, Lewes decided that the best way to simulate the two-directional movements of a proper parachute jump was to have the men leap from the back of moving Bedfords onto the hard desert floor, then roll in the direction of the lorry, which would simulate the wind movement of a real drop. At first the Bedfords travelled at a relatively safe 15mph, but as the men became more efficient, Lewes gradually doubled the speed, which made the jumps a lot more dangerous and eventually led to many accidents, including severe sprains and fractured bones.

'That Lewes is barmy,' Taff said. 'I respect him, but he's crazy. Those jumps from the Bedfords are more dangerous than real ones could possibly be. We've lost a lot of good men through them and those of us still here are black and blue. That crazy bastard will kill us all.'

'He's making the jumps as well,' Neil reminded him.

'Just shows he's mad,' Taff replied.

Nevertheless, the brutal jumps from speeding lorries continued until it was time for the remaining men to make their first jumps from an aeroplane. MEHQ had finally made a Bombay bomber available on a daily basis for this purpose; however, as Ringway was still being uncooperative, the Detachment had to rely on guesswork and self-tuition. Luckily, unlike the Valentia which had almost killed Stirling, the Bombay had a proper overhead suspension for the static line of the chutes, allowing for the use of a snap-link.

Feeling that it was necessary for him to make a showing at this point, Stirling made the first two jumps with the men. These were successful and the men were euphoric. But during the next jumps, when Stirling remained on the ground to visually check the air and landing patterns, the snap-links

attaching the static lines of the first two parachutists to the overhead suspension cable twisted, the
rings slipped free, the parachute canopies remained
in their packs, and the men plunged screaming to
their deaths.

Shocked, Stirling cancelled the rest of that day's
jumps and gave the men the day off. Nevertheless,
the jumps were ruthlessly resumed the following
morning, with Stirling setting a good example
by being the first out of the aircraft. This time
the snap-links were carefully checked and there
were no further casualties. Within a matter of
weeks the remaining men were expert, confident
paratroopers.

One major problem remained. As the main
purpose of the planned raids was to destroy
enemy aircraft and other vehicles on the ground,
as well as fuel and ammunition dumps, the men,
if using orthodox explosives, would need to hump
murderously heavy loads to their chosen targets,
then set them off almost instantly and make a
quick getaway. Given the state of contemporary
explosives, neither of these ideas was feasible:
most explosives were too heavy to carry over such
distances and the usual constituents – gelignite,
thermite and ammonal – took too long to be
ignited or exploded.

What Lewes wanted was something smaller and lighter, and therefore easier to carry. What he also wanted was a combination of the explosive and the incendiary that could be set off almost instantly. When told by a disdainful Royal Army Ordnance Corps expert that this was impossible, he studied the subject during his three busy months in Kabrit, eventually producing a blend of plastic explosive (PE) and thermite kneaded together with a lubricant into a bomb the size of a tennis ball. This explosive-inflammable mix gave a charge of about 400g.

'On the boss of a propeller,' Lewes explained to Stirling, Greaves and Callaghan, 'it will not only damage the prop itself but also set alight any petrol or other fuel within range of the blast. In other words, it's perfect for destroying grounded aircraft and other vehicles – and certainly for fuel and ammunition dumps. It's also exceptionally small and light, and so easy to carry. Last but not least, with the explosive fused in its own right and the incendiary device timed to ignite just *after* the explosion, you won't find anything quicker or more devastating.'

'I'm not sure what all that means,' Stirling said with a broad smile, 'but I'm sure it will work.'

It did. Tested in the presence of Royal Army Ordnance Corps representatives, the device was highly successful and immediately named the 'Lewes bomb'.

'Thank you kindly,' Captain Stirling said to the RAOC representatives, speaking on behalf of the man he now considered to be a modest genius. 'It's the least you can do.'

Vengeance being sweet, it was now time for L Detachment to stop practising and see some action. Stirling was well aware of the fact that the only kind of man who could pass the tests set by Lewes was the kind of man who could not easily endure boredom. This belief was confirmed when Greaves and Callaghan informed him that the men were becoming frustrated with their endless retraining in the furnace of Kabrit and wanted to put their learning to good use. As it happened, their enthusiasm coincided with General Auchinleck's first major offensive to relieve Tobruk and push Rommel's seemingly invincible Afrika Korps out of Cyrenaica.

'To aid this push,' Stirling explained to the whole detachment at a briefing convened in the mess tent, 'we will raid five forward airfields spread around Gazala and Timini. This will involve five separate raiding parties of twelve men, travelling in five aircraft and being dropped at five specific locations, well away from the targets. The drop will take place on the night of 16 November. You will march throughout the night to lying-up positions in view of the targets. From your LUPs you will observe the targets and assess their individual situations. Infiltration of the airfields, the placing of bombs and detonation will take place in the early hours of the morning. The fuses will be coordinated, as far as possible, to detonate under cover of darkness. The groups will then make a forced march before first light, back to a preselected RV to join up with the LRDG, who will return them to base. Exfiltration will be by LRDG lorry to Siwa Oasis, then back to here. Average distance from airfield to RV will be forty miles. The commanders of the five groups will be myself with Sergeant Lorrimer as second-in-command; Captain Callaghan; Lieutenant Greaves; Lieutenant Bollington; and Captain Lewes. Are there any questions?'

'Yes, boss,' Sergeant Lorrimer said after a long silence. 'When do we leave?'

'This afternoon,' answered Captain Stirling.

5

The five raiding parties boarded five Bombays late
that afternoon with a certain amount of trepida-
tion, since reports of likely ground winds of thirty
knots – almost twice the hazard level – had led
Stirling to call a last-minute Chinese parliament,
asking if the men were willing to carry on despite
the dangerous weather, which could scatter them
widely over the desert. The men were unanimous
that they should go anyway, particularly as the last
three raids planned by Layforce had been cancelled
earlier that year, leaving most of them extremely
frustrated.

'Then let's do it, lads,' Stirling said.

With packed bergens strapped under their Irvin
X-Type parachute packs, and burdened down with
a wide variety of weapons, they were heavily
laden. The weapons included 9mm Sten sub-
machine-guns, M1 Thompson sub-machine-guns,

or tommy-guns, and Bren light machine-guns. Their criss-crossed webbing was festooned with 30 and 32-round box magazines, hand-grenades, water bottles, survival kits and, of course, the brand-new Lewes bombs. Strapped to the belt around their waists were the ubiquitous 9mm Browning High Power handgun, Sykes-Fairburn commando knife, bayonet, compass and binoculars. The bergens were crammed with other items, including food, and weighed nearly 90lb on their own.

When Stirling's Bombay took off, at 1930 hours, the roar of its twin engines made conversation impossible among the twelve men sitting on the fuselage floor above the bomb racks. The lack of room was made even worse than usual by the enormous long-range fuel tank taking up the middle of the plane, down much of its length.

'Are we expecting flak on this flight?' Jimbo asked nervously.

'Yes,' Frankie replied. 'And I know just what you're thinking. If any hits that fucking fuel tank we can call it a day.'

'Too bloody right,' Jimbo said.

Though the Bombay had taken off in a clear, windless night, the weather soon deteriorated, and as they neared the target area the engines laboured more strenuously through dark storm clouds and the vibrations became worse. Shortly after they had flown into those boiling clouds, the clap of thunder was heard above the labouring engines and fingers of lightning illuminated the sky.

Even as the aircraft began to buck and shudder wildly from the storm, the sound of anti-aircraft guns was added to the bedlam and tracers began flickering past the windows, as if competing with the lightning to light up the dark sky with jagged phosphorescent lines.

'Shit!' Neil exclaimed. 'If we don't get it from the weather, we'll cop it from the flak. Let's get the fuck out of here.'

While the aircraft bucked and rolled crazily, Stirling made his way along the hold and disappeared into the captain's cabin at the front. Eventually returning to the men, some of whom were now feeling airsick, he said, 'I feel obliged to tell you that the captain's having trouble estimating the force and direction of the wind, which means he's having difficulty navigating. He dropped a sea marker flare which showed that we're off course, so he's going to attempt to use the coastline's configuration as a navigational aid. This will, of course, expose us to more anti-aircraft fire, so be prepared for the worst.'

'Fucking great!' Jimbo muttered.

The worsening vibrations of the struggling Bombay almost numbed the paratroopers' senses as they methodically checked their gear for the last time. Five minutes later, however, when the aircraft was flying through an inferno of thunder, lightning, tracers and exploding flak, it was hit by something, rocked violently, then shuddered and started descending in what was clearly not a controlled manner.

Though it was impossible to stand upright without support, Stirling again made his way along to the pilot's cabin and returned to inform his men that the aircraft had been hit by flak, but had not been badly damaged and was continuing on to the DZ, the drop zone. Lieutenant Bollington's Bombay, however, had taken a worse hit and its entire instrument panel had been shattered. It was now leaking petrol from a damaged wing tank and losing power, so the pilot planned to head back to base.

'*If* he makes it,' Neil whispered mournfully, then looked a bit alarmed as the Bombay abruptly banked steeply.

'Don't worry,' the RAF dispatcher informed the paratroopers. 'We've just banked into our inland turn. You have six minutes to zero hour. On your feet, boys and girls.'

When the men had done as they were told, the dispatcher, an RAF sergeant who would supervise the jump, checked their static lines. Designed to jerk open the chutes as each man fell clear of the aircraft, they were fixed to 'strong points' in the fuselage. A man's life could depend on them, but in this obsolete aircraft the fixings looked suspiciously flimsy. If these twisted free, the canopies would not open and the men would plunge to their deaths. However, a sharp tug on each line by the dispatcher satisfied him that the new clips would hold firm. He then moved to the door and nodded to the aircraftman to open it. When the latter did so, cold air rushed in with a startling roar.

With their senses abruptly revived by the shock of the cold, rushing air, the paratroopers lined up to make the jump. Supply packs of weapons and explosives tied to parachutes were stacked up in the rear of the fuselage, behind the lines of men, waiting to be pitched out by the airmen when the last of the paratroopers had gone; other boxes with parachutes were clipped to the bomb racks, also ready for dropping. Unable to be heard above the roar of wind and engines, the dispatcher mouthed the words 'Get ready' and pointed to the lamp above his head.

The sounds of anti-aircraft fire and exploding

flak heard a few minutes earlier as the plane had banked into its inland turn had set the men's adrenalin racing. Now, though nerves were steadier, their knowledge that the pilot was having difficulty finding the DZ, increased their fear of the unknown.

When Stirling's gaze turned towards the small lamp mounted by the doorway, his eleven companions did the same. Men eased their shoulders more comfortably into their harnesses, fidgeted with their weapons, checked their equipment yet again, and forgot the discomforts of the two and a half hours already spent in the plane. At once nervous and relieved, they now just wanted to jump, to get it over and done with.

The red light came on. Two minutes to go.

Stirling, leading the drop, was first in line, at the door, waiting for the green light. When it flashed on, the dispatcher slapped his shoulder and he threw himself out. The second man, Lorrimer, moved up to take Stirling's place and waited for a similar slap. He saw his predecessor's line snake out and jar taut for a split second, before it trailed slackly from the door. Lorrimer heard a bawled 'Go!' before he felt the signal, then he he was out in the black void, the wind of the slipstream slapping at him, its noise deafening, as he held himself upright, heels together, waiting for the slipstream to release him and let him drop vertically, which it did within seconds. A sudden jerk and the roaring wind ceased, then Lorrimer dropped down through darkness and silence, looking for the ground. Where the hell was it?

By now Stirling should have felt, or at least seen, the ground, yet the blackness seemed bottomless as he continued drifting down. Suddenly, however, as he gripped the rigging lines, preparing to swing himself clear of anything harmful, he was smashed against a rocky stretch of desert. Hitting the ground with a jolt, he rolled over and was dragged away by the fierce wind, but he managed to roll again, this time onto his stomach, meanwhile wrestling to control the rigging lines, collapsing the canopy. Breathless and battered, with darting pains shooting through him, he was snatched away again by another strong gust of wind, then bumped, cut and bruised as he was dragged at great speed over sharp rocks and abrasive gravel. Somehow he managed to punch the release box and unravel his harness. Then he passed out.

Regaining consciousness, Stirling found himself lying on his belly. Rolling onto his back, he saw patches of stars between drifting storm clouds and, below them, the pale white flowers of other parachutes descending too far away.

'Damn!' Stirling whispered.

Attempting to stand, he was almost knocked off balance by the wind. Stinging granules of rock, the so-called 'sand' of the desert, stung his face, made breathing difficult and finally forced him to turn downwind, into the desert.

The gale had blown for several hours and put the other paratroopers well beyond their intended DZ, but Stirling did not know that just yet. He expected to find the rest of his party downwind. But when he reached what should have been the DZ, not one man was in sight.

Stirling was all on his own, lost in the desert, in the middle of the raging sandstorm that had reduced visibility to almost zero.

After fighting to get his breath back, gritting his teeth against the pain of his many cuts and bruises, and checking that his bergen straps and webbing were in one piece, Stirling switched on his torch and headed resolutely into the dark, storm-lashed desert.

Fighting against the raging storm and almost blind in the darkness, Stirling marched in the direction of where he thought he had seen the other paratroopers. Though shouting his name constantly, his words were lost in the wind, so he shone his torch left and right as a beacon, hoping someone would see it. Eventually, after what seemed like an eternity, he saw the light of another torch veering from side to side, then another, and at last heard voices calling out to him. He soon came face to face with Ashman and Turner, both smeared with a film of sand and dust, leaning into the howling wind.

'Have you seen anyone else?' Stirling bawled.

Private Ashman nodded and pointed west. 'Yes!' he bawled back. 'Over there! About half a mile away.'

'Let's go and find them!' Stirling bawled.

Heading in that direction, the three men managed to link up with two others in the group, Lorrimer and Moffatt, then the search for the others continued, with all the men yelling out their names and waving their torches. In this manner it took nearly two hours for ten of the original group to link up. The eleventh man, Corporal Tanner, was missing and a further two hours of searching failed to find him.

'He was probably dragged out into the desert,' Stirling ventured with a sinking heart. 'Almost certainly that's what happened, likewise to the ten packages of weapons that were dropped.'

'There's two of them over there,' Frankie Turner said, pointing east. 'In the bed of a wadi. I didn't see any more.'

'Let's go and fetch them,' a dispirited Stirling said.

One of the parachuted crates contained Lewes bombs without fuses. There were also a few rations, but only enough for one day, and twelve water bottles, containing in all just over two gallons of drinking water.

'Fat lot of good this will do us,' Lorrimer said as they squatted on the cold wadi bed, protected from the howling wind but still covered in swirling sand, nibbling at some of the rations and quenching their thirst with the water. 'No weapons apart from our pistols. No explosives. Nothing. We can't do a damned thing, boss.'

'We can at least have a look at the enemy installations,' Stirling said stubbornly, refusing to go back empty-handed.

'I'm willing,' Lorrimer said, understanding Stirling's frustration, 'but I don't think we should put the men through that after this bloody disaster.'

'But you'll come with me?'

'Yes, boss.'

Stirling checked his watch by the light of his

torch. 'Three hours to daylight,' he said. 'That should give us enough time.'

'Just about,' Lorrimer agreed.

Stirling called Sergeant Bob Tappman over to tell him what they had planned. 'Our objective,' he said, 'is the German airfield near Gazala in Cyrenaica – one of the five we were to raid in this area. It should have been only a few hours' march from here, so although we can no longer raid it Sergeant Lorrimer and I are going to have a look at it while you take the remaining men direct to the rendezvous with the LRDG lorries. If we're at the correct DZ, the RV should be less than 30 miles away.'

'*If* we're at the correct DZ,' Tappman said bitterly.

Stirling shrugged. 'What is there to lose?'

Tappman returned to the men crouched on the dark floor of the wadi, grateful for its protection from the freezing, howling wind. When he had conveyed the news to them, they climbed wearily, dispiritedly to their feet, fell into single file and clambered up out of the wadi one by one, gradually disappearing into the stormy night. When they had all gone, Stirling and Lorrimer likewise climbed out and headed in what they assumed was the direction of Gazala.

They marched through the cold and dark until the grey light of dawn broke, when they laid up for a short break and a few nibbles of their remaining food. They then continued the march, taking their bearings from the Trig El Abd, a track line in the desert, previously used by the camel trains of the slave trade, then by either Axis or Allied vehicles, depending on who was holding the area.

After a hike of about ten miles, with the weather changing again and returning to a fierce, dry heat that lasted until last light, they reached a featureless desert plateau that led to an escarpment: a line of cliffs from which they could see the Mediterranean beyond the coast road. The road itself was the military supply route (MSR) for German and Italian forces loosely holding a line from the sea at Sollum, on the Egyptian border, 120 miles to the east of Gazala, well beyond the Allied enclave at Tobruk. Seeing the MSR, and the constant flow of Axis traffic heading along it in both directions, they realized that they had been dropped well south of their intended DZ, only ten miles or so from the coast.

'There's no airfield here,' Lorrimer said, lying flat on his belly beside Stirling on the escarpment and studying the MSR through his binoculars. 'We're miles away, boss.'

'Then let's not waste our journey,' Stirling replied stubbornly. 'We'll stay here for a bit and gather as much info as we can on the troop movements along that route. That at least will be something.'

'Yes, boss,' Lorrimer sighed wearily.

Unfortunately they were foiled in even that simple plan. They laid up all night and recced the MSR the following morning, but late that afternoon black clouds formed in the sky and they knew that another storm was coming. Hoping to find shelter, they advanced the last four miles to the edge of the escarpment, where they took shelter in a dried-up wadi bed, which they planned to use as their observation post (OP).

This was a mistake. When the clouds broke in a deluge of rain, they were caught unawares in the last thing that newcomers to the desert expect to encounter – a 'flash flood.' As the rain poured down with the force of a tropical storm, hitting the sand like bullets and making it spit and splash as mud, the bed of the wadi gradually filled up with water, becoming first a stream, then a fast-flowing river. This forced the pair to clamber up out of the wadi, where they were exposed to the full force of the storm, lashed by a freezing wind and now drenched completely by the torrential, incredibly noisy rain. Even as they lay there, hardly believing what they were experiencing, the river in the wadi became a raging torrent that swept baked sand and gravel along with it as it took the line of least resistance and roared along between the high banks of the wadi.

To make matters worse, the storm and flash floods – the latter were deluging other wadis – had blotted out the landscape and made surveillance of the MSR impossible. It was now clear to Stirling that their presence here could serve no valid purpose.

'There's no alternative but to head for the RV,' he said, sounding bitterly disappointed, even though the storm was starting to abate. 'And I think we should start straight away, before another storm comes.'

'No argument,' Lorrimer said.

The RV, they knew, lay 40 miles inland, back along the Trig El Abd. Luckily, as the rain was still falling, they were able to fill up their water bottles before leaving. When they did eventually set off, the rain was still falling, they were thoroughly soaked, and Stirling's beloved, carefully packed cigarettes had virtually disintegrated in his sodden kit.

'I can't bear to be without a smoke,' he said. 'That's worse than anything else.'

Lorrimer laughed at that.

Again they marched throughout the night. In the early hours of the morning, about three hours before first light, Lorrimer realized that he could barely put his weight on his swollen ankle, twisted during his parachute landing but passing virtually unnoticed in the tension generated by their many arduous, dangerous activities since the drop. Now it hurt like hell. Nevertheless, he followed Stirling steadily in the direction which the latter had judged would bring them to the RV where, it was hoped, the LRDG's A patrol would be shining a Tilley lamp from a small hill as a welcoming beacon.

By 0700 the next morning, they had been over 36 hours in the desert. When the rain stopped, about dawn, they slumped in the shade of a hillock and slept the sleep of the dead for four hours. Their wet clothes had dried on them before they moved off again in the midday haze. By then the heat was fierce, scorching their skin, blistering their lips and filling them with an unceasing thirst that compelled them to finish off the water they had gathered from the rainfall on the escarpment the previous day.

Late that afternoon, just as they were both starting to feel that they might go mad from thirst, the weather turned yet again, becoming much cooler and, more importantly, bringing back the rain and enabling them to fill their bottles. Replenished and cooled down after their long, thirsty journey through the fierce heat, they continued the arduous march across the scorched, barren waste.

They were some 12 miles from the RV when Stirling spotted movement far to the south. Through his binoculars he made out nine figures heading for the Trig El Abd.

'Nine men,' he said to Lorrimer, 'heading westward. It can only be Sergeant Tappman and the others. Let's hope they make it the rest of the way without being caught.'

'Let's hope *we* do,' Lorrimer said sardonically, still limping badly when he walked, but marching on anyway.

Stirling and Lorrimer marched throughout a third night, stopping only to watch a sudden, fierce sandstorm blowing up in the distance, where they had seen the other nine men.

'Poor bastards,' Sergeant Lorrimer murmured.

When the sandstorm had abated, they marched on again, finally lying up in the early hours of the morning, dropping off almost immediately and once more sleeping like dead men.

On waking just before first light, they saw what they thought was a star very low in the sky. But when they continued their march and drew closer to the glowing object, they realized that it was A Patrol's lamp shining in the south, no more than two or three miles away.

They had made it back.

An exhausted Stirling and a badly limping Lorrimer found the LRDG lorries hidden under camouflage nets in a small ravine. There they were welcomed with hot tea laced with whisky, which perked them up temporarily. They were further buoyed up to find Lieutenant Greaves and Captain Lewes already at the RV with eight of their ten men. They, too, had had a disastrous drop and been up to the coast to fix their position before marching to this RV. Likewise Paddy Callaghan, who had come in just before Stirling and Lorrimer, having waited nearby to be sure that he had correctly identified the position of the patrol.

But Stirling's brief euphoria was dashed when Callaghan told him what had happened to his group.

'By the time we reached our DZ, much later than your lot, we found ourselves parachuting down through winds blowing at 90 mph. You can imagine! A lot of the men were injured as they landed, others were lost, and the rest of us, having no choice, marched on into the desert as planned, though with most of our weapons and supplies missing. The storm didn't let up. More men were lost. Another had a fatal heart attack. After that I accepted that our situation was hopeless and led the remaining men towards the coast. When I reached there, I used the configuration of the coastline to navigate my way back to the RV. No enemy airfields were sighted, let alone sabotaged, and I lost eighty per cent of my men. A complete disaster, I fear.'

'Has anything else been heard of the Bombay that was damaged and tried to limp back to base?'

'Lieutenant Bollington's plane?' Callaghan looked none too happy. 'According to Captain Owen, commander of this LRDG group, Bollington was captured with his men. The damaged Bombay made a forced landing west of Tobruk. The crew made emergency repairs and took off again, but they were forced to crash-land for a second time after being attacked by an Me 109F. That's when they were captured – all twelve of them, plus the air crew.'

'Damn!' Stirling growled.

He was further deflated when he found Privates Ashman, Turner and Moffatt huddled together against the wheels of a lorry, covered with sand and gravel, red-eyed, clearly exhausted, and comforting themselves with tea and whisky.

'You men look like you've had a rough time,' Stirling said. 'What happened out there?'

Turner and Moffatt glanced at Jimbo, who then spoke up for all of them. 'When we left the DZ we soon learnt that we'd been dropped far off the mark.'

'Yes,' Stirling interjected impatiently, 'I found that out as well.'

'So,' Jimbo continued, ignoring the interruption, 'we couldn't find our bearings and got even more lost. To make matters worse, we then ran into winds of over 90 mph . . .'

'You as well!' Stirling murmured bitterly.

'. . . and a lot of us then lost one another and were widely scattered. We three' – Jimbo nodded, indicating Turner and Moffatt – 'found ourselves still with Sergeant Tappman, who managed to lead us out of the storm. We were looking for the Trig El Abd, but just before last light we turned in the wrong direction and instead ran into a Kraut patrol. There was a brief fire-fight – we only had our Browning handguns – and Sergeant Tappman deliberately exposed himself to the Krauts, distracting them, while we made our escape along a wadi bed. We saw him being captured and taken away. Eventually, we made our way back to the Trig El Abd, which eventually led us back here. A good bloke, that Tappman.'

When the figures were calculated the results were truly shocking. Totting up those captured, missing or presumed dead, it became clear to Stirling that of the original sixty-two men, only twenty-two had made it back.

Dispirited and badly shaken, though not yet defeated, Stirling and the remainder of his men were driven back to the base at Kabrit by the LRDG.

6

The LRDG took Captain Stirling and his twenty-one men to Siwa Oasis, nearly 200 miles to the south-west and across the frontier, at the crossroads of the old caravan routes. With its salt-water lake, fierce dry heat, and swarms of black flies, Siwa was noted for its ability to tax a man's strength and destroy his will to work. For this very reason Stirling had no desire to leave his men there very long.

All the same, it was a beautiful place. Seven miles long and two miles wide, it was abundant with water and palm trees. Beyond the palm groves, to the south, rolled the great white dunes, running north to south in the Great Sand Sea. An area approximately the same size as Ireland, it could only be crossed 130 miles south of Siwa by a route that passed the artesian well at Ain Dalla, the last watering-hole in over 300 miles en route for Kufra.

To the north-west of Siwa lay the Quattra Depression, running further northward to stop only 50 yards from the sea near El Alamein. Unfortunately, its floor was so far below sea level that it was impassable to ordinary vehicles.

A month after arriving at Siwa, bored and frustrated, Stirling managed to arrange a meeting with Brigadier D.W. Reid, in the Jalo Oasis garrison, nearly 250 miles away. There, in the brigadier's tent, Stirling got down to business.

'Kufra is the key settlement to the control of the inner desert,' he promptly informed Reid. 'Over 1000 miles from the coast and stretching for some 1300 miles from the Nile westward – an area about the size of the Indian subcontinent.'

'True,' Reid said, topping up his tea with whisky and looking up to see if Stirling wanted the same. When Stirling nodded, the brigadier also laced his tea with whisky, then sat back on his dusty wooden chair. 'Unfortunately, it's haunted by the ghibli . . .'

'Pardon?'

'A hot wind laden with dust, rather than sand,' Reid explained. 'In fact, true sandstorms are rare in these parts, though duststorms, as you well know, occur frequently and can be devastating. The ghibli is even worse. Also, the great variation in temperature inland – fifty degrees by noon, frost in the morning – can lead ill-equipped or irresolute men to die from exposure. In short, the Great Sand Sea was well named when the Arabs dubbed it the Devil's Country. It's a murderous terrain for all but them.'

'Yet some SAS men,' Stirling said, not missing his opportunity, 'crossed that desert without boots, water or even rations, in their determination to survive. That's why, despite the failure of our first raid, we have to try it again.'

Brigadier Reid smiled, admiring Stirling's tenacity, the more so because it was a virtue he possessed himself. Indeed, even as Stirling was being brought into Siwa by the LRDG, Reid had been leading his 'Oasis' force with great skill and tenacity to take Aujila and then capture the 600 Italians of the Jalo garrison, despite a dreadful pounding from Axis aircraft. His tenacity, and that of his men, had finally won the day.

Now, here in Jalo, the former trading centre of the Majabra Arabs, he was deciding whether or not he should help Stirling in his bid to return to the desert for another series of raids in which LRDG patrols would also be used. Their FOB, or forward operating base, had been set up around the few sand-blown huts and Italian buildings which were all that remained of this once prosperous settlement. But it was ideal for L Detachment's purpose: raids which would destroy German aircraft at Agedabia and elsewhere on the coastline of the Gulf of Sirte.

'I still have my doubts about whether you should try this again,' Reid said, easing his massive frame into his chair and puffing out his bright red cheeks to blow a stream of blue smoke from his cigar. 'Nor am I alone in this. MEHQ also has doubts. There's even been talk of pulling you out of the field altogether. Sorry to be so blunt, dear boy, but those are the facts.'

Recalling his sodden cigarettes on the escarpment over the MSR that ran from Sollum to Gazala, Stirling was smoking with relish now while his brain worked overtime. He had always known that there were those among the gabardine swine who wanted to have L Detachment 22 SAS disbanded altogether, so he was hardly shocked to hear the brigadier confirm it. Nevertheless, he had to make his move now, before the voices of his enemies gained sway. Luckily, he had an ace up his sleeve: his old supporter, General Ritchie, the former Deputy Chief of General Staff, Cairo, who had since been placed in command of the Eighth Army.

'I don't mind your bluntness, Denys, and I accept what you're saying, but not *everyone* at MEHQ is against me. In fact, General Ritchie still had great faith in the enterprise – even more so, given the tenacity displayed by my men in that desert after the first raid, irrespective of the failure of the raid itself. I'm sure he'll support us.'

Reid smiled again and revealed his pleasant surprise. 'I knew that all along, David. In fact, I spoke to Ritchie about it. Ritchie in turn spoke to the C-in-C. Auchinleck's not only prepared to let you continue your raids, but is giving you a free hand to plan the details.'

At this news Stirling felt a great surge of joy well up inside him. In truth, he had been suffering a deepening sense of failure and despair since the disaster in the Gazala area and wished to repair the damage as soon as possible. The damage was not only to the reputation of the new-born L Detachment, but to the morale of the individual men. Many of them had been deeply shocked by the loss of friends during the disastrous parachute drop and afterwards. Others had taken the failure personally and were blaming themselves for it. Those negative feelings had not been eased by their month in Siwa Oasis, where they had little to do but endlessly retrain to keep an edge to their skills. Apart from the retraining, which bored most of them anyway, they had too much time to brood on the widely discussed failure of the first raids and its effect on the reputation of L Detachment. This doubtless explained why tempers were short and fisticuffs not infrequent during the evenings. Already many had asked to be sent back to Kabrit, which was at least nearer to Cairo, but so far Stirling had refused. He had his reasons.

'That's wonderful news,' he said to Brigadier Reid, puffing streams of cigarette smoke between each precisely placed word. 'I'm really thrilled, Denys.'

'Naturally,' Reid replied, 'since all of your few remaining trained men will be needed in the field, I'll be happy to help you overcome your supply problems until you decide on a parent organization for L Detachment.'

'I've already decided,' Stirling said. 'I want it to be the LRDG.'

Reid nodded, puffed another cloud of cigar smoke, then flicked the ash into his ashtray with a surprisingly elegant movement of his large hand. 'A good choice. L Detachment and the LRDG are natural allies, involved in similar business and operating virtually the same way. You can learn a lot from the LRDG.'

'I've always been happy to take their advice.'

'That's why you work well together.'

The field telephone on the brigadier's desk – actually a trestle table – gave a loud, jangling ring. The brigadier picked the phone up, listened briefly, then put it down and smiled at Stirling.

'Major Steele has arrived,' he said, rising as someone entered the tent behind Stirling. Standing up and turning around, Stirling found himself face to face with Major Don Steele of the LRDG. The two men shook hands.

'Delighted to meet you at last, old chap,' Steele said, taking the chair beside Stirling, facing Reid. 'I've heard a lot about that last op and was very impressed.'

'The last op was a failure,' Stirling said, 'that brought me a lot of flak.'

Steele grinned. 'I'm sure it did. There are, however, lessons to be learnt from failure. Though the raids were not successful, your men performed magnificently. Their hikes across an average of 50 miles of desert to the RV have already become almost legendary. Never mind the sceptics of MEHQ. L Detachment has nothing to be ashamed of and a lot to be proud of.'

'It's a relief to hear that,' Stirling said, meaning

it, liking Steele immensely. 'The failure hit the men hard.'

'You won't fail this time.'

'Now that the backslapping is finished,' Reid said tartly, 'can we get down to business?'

Steele grinned again. 'Yes, sir.'

Reid stood and went to the covered blackboard raised up behind his desk. After picking up a pointer, he removed the canvas sheet covering the blackboard, to reveal a large map of the Cyrenaica Desert.

'While your good friend General Ritchie has recently been reinforced,' he said, 'the Axis forces are short of men and supplies – mainly because the Allies now control the Mediterranean. This is a situation which Ritchie wants to exploit. He intends reaching Derna by 19 December and, with forward elements of the 22nd Guards Brigade, be 10 miles east of Benghazi by the 23rd.'

'Ambitious,' Stirling said. 'What's our role?'

Reid tapped the word 'Agedabia' with his pointer. It was on the coast, approximately 120 miles north of Jalo Oasis and 75 miles south of Benghazi. 'My Flying Squadron is under orders to link up with Brigadier Marriott's force in this area and be in position by 22 December, in support of the Allied advance on Benghazi. My problem in doing this

is the threat from the German aircraft at ...'
He tapped the names off, one by one, with
his pointer. '... Agedabia, Sirte and Agheila.
Your job is to remove that threat before we
move out.'

Stirling nodded, then stood up. He went to the
map and studied it carefully.

'My suggestion,' Steele said carefully behind him,
'is that you take as few men as possible – though
enough to do the job – and, instead of parachuting
in, let us take you on LRDG vehicles to within
striking distance of Sirte.'

'Why Sirte?' Stirling asked, still studying the map
covering the blackboard.

'It's considered to be the most important,' Reid
replied.

Stirling nodded again, inhaled on his cigarette,
studied the map with his cheeks puffed out, then
blew out a cloud of smoke and turned back to face
the other two officers.

'Right,' he said firmly, having decided. 'I'll move
out with Paddy Callaghan and ten men on 10
December, targeting Sirte. Captain Lewes will
be assigned to Agheila, moving out on the 9th.
Both groups will attack on the night of the 14th.
Finally, Lieutenant Greaves will target Agedabia,
in support of your move ...' Stirling nodded,

indicating Reid. '. . . Greaves will move out on the 18th to make his attack on the 21st. By the time you advance, Denys, the airfields should all be out of action.'

'Let's hope so,' Reid said.

'This time I have no doubts,' Stirling told him. 'My men are ready, willing and able. They'll do a good job.'

'With good support from us,' Steele said. 'Of that you can rest assured.'

'More mutual backslapping,' Reid said sardonically, relighting his cigar and belching out more smoke. 'May I remind you, gentlemen, that actions speak louder than words.'

'You'll get all the action you want,' Steele said with a wide, boyish grin. 'Of *that* you can rest assured!'

'We're gonna hang out our washing on the Siegfried Line,' Stirling said, quoting the lyrics of the morale-boosting song. 'And it will all start right here in North Africa.'

The three men chuckled at that, then Stirling left his fellow officers in the tent and marched enthusiastically across the sun-scorched oasis, with its cool water and palm trees, to raise the spirits of his men with what he regarded as exceptionally good news.

THE DESERT RAIDERS

He was not surprised, when he told them what was going to happen, that the men cheered and applauded for several minutes.

7

'So those are the targets,' Stirling said, completing his summary of the forthcoming operations at a briefing in a large tent pitched in the shade of a grove of palm trees, close to the glittering water of the Jalo Oasis. The men had arrived there the day before, after a long, hot drive in lorries over the Great Sand Sea from Siwa Oasis. 'This time, however, instead of parachuting in from Bombays, we'll be driven in by the LRDG.'

A disgruntled murmuring made Stirling glance uneasily at Major Steele, who was sitting in a chair beside him, behind the long trestle table, directly facing Captain Lewes, Captain Callaghan, and Lieutenant Greaves. All three officers were sitting in the front row of hard chairs with the rest of L Detachment seated behind them and Sergeant Lorrimer, his thick arms crossed on his broad chest, standing at the back of the tent, keeping a beady eye on his increasingly frustrated, contentious men.

'Before any of you start complaining,' Stirling said, waving them into attentive silence, 'please let it be noted that the LRDG, apart from their exemplary reconnaissance and intelligence-gathering work, have actually paved the way for the kind of raids we're planning to launch. Indeed, only last week ... Well, I'll let Major Steele tell the story.'

Looking surprisingly nervous, the normally polished Major Steele pushed his chair back, stood up and cleared his throat.

'In late November,' he said, 'the Eighth Army was embroiled in a battle with Axis forces between Sollum and Tobruk. Two LRDG patrols, G1 and G2, were ordered to intercept transport on the road running 70 miles north from Agedabia to the main Axis base at Benghazi.'

'Big deal!' Frankie Turner whispered contemptuously to his good friend Jimbo Ashman, though not loud enough for Steele to hear.

'The patrols were attacked from the air when nearing the coast,' the major continued, 'but the commander of G1, Captain Tony Hay, led his patrol in an attack at dusk on the 28th against a roadside eating house located about 30 miles south of Benghazi. His eight vehicles, having driven several miles down the main road under heavy air attack, turned into the parking area and fired armour-piercing and incendiary bullets from their machine-guns. While they were doing so, a man on each lorry lobbed grenades at some thirty Axis vehicles. The patrol then escaped in the gathering darkness.'

Always willing to listen to a tale of derring-do, the SAS men, though in a contentious mood, gave Steele breathing space. He used it to cough into his fist, clearing a throat made dry by self-consciousness, then gamely continued.

'The men of G1 weren't followed, but after lying up next day in the desert, they returned to the road at dusk to shoot up a fuel tanker, killing its driver and passenger, forcing it off the road. The rest of the Axis drivers then fled back in the directions they had come from while the LRDG vehicles drove back into the safety of the desert – again unmolested.'

Taff Clayton yawned melodramatically, pretending to hide it with his hand, only removing his hand from his face to ask: 'So? Did they make it back?'

'Yes,' Steele answered, suddenly showing a little mettle, or perhaps anger, in his formerly shaky voice. 'After spending the rest of that night in the desert, they spent a further day near the road, but were recalled and reached Siwa on 3 December.'

When Stirling saw the blank faces of his men, most of whom thought of themselves as a cut above the average, including the LRDG, he straightened his shoulders, which made him look even taller, and said forcefully: 'The point we wish to make is that that LRDG raid, and others just like it, forced the enemy to withdraw troops from the main battle area to protect his lines of communication – a ploy we are now going to exploit to the full with the invaluable help of the LRDG, who have, incidentally, thankfully already paved the way for us.'

Stirling nodded appreciatively in the direction of Steele while some of the more dissenting SAS men rolled their eyeballs or shook their heads from side to side in disbelief.

'Any questions so far?' Sergeant Lorrimer bawled.

'No, Sarge!' some of the men shouted back.

'Then stop all that whispering and fidgeting and listen to your CO!'

'Yes, Sarge!' they shouted back in unison.

'All right, men, all right,' Stirling said with a grin, raising his big hands to silence them. 'Fun time is over.' When they had settled down, he continued: 'Now that the proper briefing is over, we'd like you to take the opportunity to ask Major Steele anything you want to know about the LRDG. Only sensible questions, please!' He cast his gaze left and right, along the rows of seated men, then to the back of the tent where Lorrimer had put his hand in the air to set the ball rolling. 'Yes, Sergeant?'

'What does the LRDG consist of, precisely? I think we're all a bit vague about that,' Lorrimer asked, looking round for confirmation.

'At present we consist of ten patrols,' Major Steele informed him. 'Each of those has the use of modified four-wheel-drive Ford F60 cars and 30 cwt Chevrolet lorries with a single tank range of 1100 miles. We have a survey section, where we make up our own maps. We have our own artillery section with a 4.5-inch howitzer, an 88mm 25-pounder, and a light tank, each mounted on a ten-tonner. We have an air section with two American WACO light aircraft purchased by the War Office. Last but not least, we have a heavy section of three-ton supply lorries, and a Light Aid Detachment for vehicle maintenance. In short, we're a self-sustaining outfit and we're well equipped.'

'Above or below?' Jimbo whispered to Frankie, who had to stifle his coarse laughter.

'What was that?' Steele asked sternly.

'Nothing, boss! Please continue.'

'Thank you, soldier, I will.' Steele stared steadily

at Jimbo for a moment, then shook his head in disgust and continued.

'The first LRDG patrol, formed by Major, now Colonel, Bagnold, had two officers and thirty other ranks with eleven vehicles, each carrying a single machine-gun, supplemented by an early Bofors – a 37mm used as an anti-tank gun – and four Boyes anti-tank rifles. Those and subsequent patrols, including G1 and G2 from the Guards Brigade, spent last summer patrolling from this oasis and Kufra, and their experiences led to a number of fundamental developments in our techniques and roles. Our job was traffic surveillance on the Axis coast a good distance away from the main battle area. We also dropped and picked up agents for the Secret Service, recced terrain which the enemy might have to cross, and occasionally raided enemy transport convoys. Our new role is to be a taxi service for you lot.'

This encouraged cheers and jeers from the men, which Sergeant Lorrimer subdued by bawling: 'Shut your mouths you lot and only speak when you've an intelligent question to ask!' The laughter tailed off into helpless chuckling, then even that died away as they felt Lorrimer breathing down their necks.

'So what were these changes in technique then?' Jimbo asked to fill the ensuing silence.

'They were related mainly to the size of patrols,' Steele replied. 'By that September we'd split the patrols into fifteen or eighteen-man teams led by an officer, with five vehicles. Our methods of crossing soft sand and navigating thousands of miles in featureless desert had improved, but they were still based on relatively simple ideas pioneered by Major Bagnold in Africa in the 1930s.'

'Which were?' Frankie Turner asked.

'Bagnold developed the steel channel strips laid for vehicles to cross soft sand. In fact, he first did this in the Sinai Desert in 1926, where he used corrugated iron. By the early 1940s all vehicles carried such channels in the desert.'

'Anything else?' Taff Clayton asked, practically yawning.

'Yes. As you probably know . . .'

'Probably!' Neil Moffatt called out from the back.

'. . . it's difficult to set up a prismatic compass in a motorized vehicle as you invariably get magnetic interference from tool-boxes and other movable metal parts.'

'I was right,' Moffatt crowed. 'We all know that!'

'Are you being funny, soldier?' Lorrimer bellowed.

'No, Sarge!' Moffatt replied.

'Then shut up and listen!'

Ignoring both of them, Steele continued: 'To use a prismatic compass in a motorized vehicle, the navigator has to get out and walk far enough away to be clear of the car's magnetic field. Even then, the compass can be an inaccurate guide – sometimes up to 400 yards out on a 20-mile march.

'Doesn't sound much to me,' Taff Clayton said.

'It's equivalent to four and a half miles adrift after a 400-mile drive. I'd say that's a lot.'

'So what did old Bagnold do?' Jimbo asked, blowing a cloud of smoke from his Woodbine.

'Major Bagnold had his navigators use a sun compass with its horizontal disc marked off in degrees and a central needle casting a shadow – rather like a sundial. The graduated disc was mounted in the car, to be rotated as the sun moved across the sky; the needle's shadow then fell to indicate the bearing on which the car was travelling. By reading the milometer, the navigator could work out his position along this bearing.'

'You've got to hand it to the LRDG,' Frankie said. 'They sure as hell know their science!'

'But even this method wasn't infallible,' Steele

continued, refusing to be drawn into this unusual detachment's verbal sparring which, so he had been informed by Stirling, was encouraged to bond the other ranks to the officers. Steele had his doubts, but was wisely keeping them to himself. 'So each night,' he continued, 'the navigator would take star bearings to fix the car's position.'

'How?' Sergeant Lorrimer asked in a perfectly normal tone of voice.

'By calculating the longitude and latitude with the aid of a theodolite and astro-navigation tables.'

'Very bright!' Jimbo said.

'Brighter than you are, soldier,' Major Steele came straight back, getting into the swing of things. 'Any more questions?'

'How do the different patrols keep in touch?'

'A sensible question from Sergeant Lorrimer,' Steele teased, then turned serious again. 'Each patrol has a radio truck with a No 11 set, which has a range of about 20 miles, and a separate set to pick up the BBC's time signals.'

'Here's an intelligent question from the other ranks,' Jimbo said. 'What about communications in general from deep in the desert?'

Steele nodded, smiling. 'It's not bad. The radio operators are able to pick up Morse from a background slush of atmospherics when working at ranges beyond the normal operational limits of the No 11 set. Their radio links from patrols to the LRDG's forward base and from the base to MEHQ in Cairo, and to the Eighth Army, are more tenuous. These operate on ground aerials at frequencies which mean that sometimes a patrol can't contact base until it's about 300 miles along its route. Our radio procedures, however, follow French civilian routines. Invariably, this makes those listening in think they're hearing a commercial station in Turkey communicating with ships in the Levant. Certainly it appears to have deceived the German radio-interception services. Because of this, our operators are able to transmit for relatively long periods at night, over great distances, without being identified or interfered with.'

'Water?' someone asked sensibly.

'I thought you heroes only drank beer,' Steele responded.

'We drink piss if we have to,' Jimbo said, 'but not if water's available.'

Steele laughed, glancing at the grinning Stirling, then answered the question. 'A gallon per man per day for all purposes, including the topping up of the individual's vehicle. No shaving permitted.'

This last encouraged an outburst of cheering and clapping. When Steele had managed to coax the men back into silence, he said: 'Once the briefing's over, I'll be taking you out and introducing you to the men designated as your "taxi drivers". Treat them with respect. Like yourselves, the LRDG has suffered a number of losses recently. In January, a soldier formerly of the Egyptian Survey Department, and one of our most valuable men, was captured along with seven of his patrol. Y Patrol lost all its officers and G Patrol lost five trucks. In short, they've been through some hard times and don't need too much ragging from you lot.'

'I would appreciate it, men,' Stirling interjected, 'if you would take those particular remarks seriously. I want no nonsense between L Detachment and the LRDG. Those men deserve your respect.'

When Steele glanced at him, he smiled and nodded, indicating that his colleague should continue.

'My men are more than mere taxi drivers,' Steele said. 'In fact, their job is to teach you everything they know about the desert – and since they're mostly old hands who've been in the desert for years, both here and in Africa, they certainly know as much as anyone about the place – perhaps even as much as the Arabs. They've learnt to live hard, carrying the minimum amount of food and water, and to read the tracks of other men, vehicles and camels in what you might think is smooth sand. They can teach you all this and more.'

Sobered by these remarks, the men remained silent until Taff Clayton put his hand up and, at a nod from Steele, asked: 'What do the various initials of the LRDG patrols stand for?'

'When Bagnold was recruiting for the LRDG he first took on a large contingent of New Zealanders, followed by Rhodesians, then a bunch from the Guards Brigade, and, finally, from all over the place. He therefore divided them into lettered patrols: S Patrol for Southern Rhodesians, G Patrol for Guards, Y Patrol for Yeomanry, and so on. It's as simple as that.'

He glanced briefly at each of the men in turn, then asked, 'Any more questions?' Seeing only a sea of shaking heads, he checked his watch, then looked up again and said, 'Right. Go and have a brew-up and be back here in exactly twenty minutes. By that time the vehicles will be here and you can commence your basic desert training.' However, just before they were dismissed, Taff Clayton put up his hand again.

'Yes?' Steele asked.

'According to what you're telling us,' Clayton said, 'we seem to have an awful lot to learn. How much time do we have?'

'Three days,' Steele answered. 'That just about gives you time for your brew-up, so you better go and get it.'

Taken aback by the tightness of the schedule, the men hurriedly filed out of the tent. When they had gone, the remaining officers – Steele, Stirling, Lewes, Callaghan and Greaves – gazed at one another in an uneasy silence that was finally broken by Steele.

'Do you really think they can do it in three days?' he asked, looking concerned.

'They had better,' Captain Stirling replied curtly. 'If they don't, we go anyway.'

He stood up and walked out.

8

What the men did not realize when they returned
from their brew-up and smoko was that their
three-day programme of training was going to
take place in the desert, by day and by night,
beginning the minute they climbed into the LRDG
vehicles. These they found waiting for them in the
scorching heat of noon when they returned from the
relative shelter of the large mess tent. The vehicles
were modified Chevrolet four-wheel-drive lorries
armed with a Boyes anti-tank rifle fixed to the rear
and a pintle-mounted Browning M1919 machine-
gun operated by the steel-helmeted front passenger.
They were covered in dust, badly battered and, in
some cases, peppered with bullet holes.

'Now you know what we're in for,' Jimbo con-
fided to his mates. 'A bleedin' suicide mission!'

After being assigned their vehicles, the men were
rekitted with clothes favoured by the LRDG for

use in the desert: shirt, shorts, Arab headgear and special sandals. The headgear consisted of a black woollen *agal*, a small hat, and a *shemagh*, a shawl with tie thongs, which went around the head, flapped in the wind, kept the face cool, and also protected the nose and mouth in a sandstorm. Normal Army boots were useless because they filled up with sand, so they were replaced with a special kind of sandal, the Indian North-West Frontier *chappli*, originally chosen by Bagnold and obtained from the Palestine Police stores. Worn with rolled-down socks, the *chappli* was particularly tough and had a hole in the toe, enabling the wearer to kick out any sand that got in without having to stop when on the march. Also supplied were funnel-shaped leather gauntlets, which stopped sweat from running down the arms and onto the weapons.

Once dressed properly, they were then able to fix to their belts the obligatory holstered 9mm Browning High Power handgun and Fairburn-Sykes commando knife. They were then loaded up with a selection of larger weapons, including the Lee-Enfield .303-inch bolt-action rifle, the 9mm Sten sub-machine-gun, the heavier M1 Thompson sub-machine-gun, and two machine-guns: the Bren light machine-gun and the Browning 0.5-inch.

'What the fuck do we need all these for?' Jimbo asked, 'if we're only learning about desert survival?'

'You'll find out,' Corporal Mick 'Monkey' Madson of the LRDG told him. 'Now get back to the transport.'

After being led back to the modified Chevrolet lorries, the men were broken up into small groups of two or three and each group assigned to a vehicle. When they had placed their weapons on the back seats, piled up around the fixed tripod-mounted Boyes anti-tank rifles, they were given a thorough briefing on the unusual vehicles. These, apart from their bristling weapons, were also fitted with reinforced sand tyres, special filters, larger fans and radiators, wireless sets, sun compasses, sextants, sand shovels, jerrycans, water condensers, woven sand mats and steel sand channels, the latter two to be used when the vehicle became trapped in deep sand.

Once a cursory summary of the vehicle's armaments had been dispensed – 'cursory' because Monkey knew that these men were familiar with such weapons – they were given a quick lesson in the use of the sun compass fixed to the vehicle's bonnet and familiarized with the workings of the sextant. They were then shown how to improvise a simple compass by stretching a string from the bonnet up to a row of nails on top of the cabin – in the case of a Bedford QL four-wheel-drive lorry – or, in the case of the Chevrolets, to another string with hooks stretched taut between the side supports of what had been the windscreen.

'Every hour,' Monkey informed them, tugging lightly at the fixed line of cord, 'you switch the string one notch along.' He removed the knotted end of cord from one of the nails hooked, in this case, to the cord strung between the windscreen uprights, and looped it over the hook beside it. 'The driver simply follows the line of the shadow created by the string and that keeps him in the right direction.'

The men were then shown how water could be conserved from the radiator. In this instance, when the water boiled, it was not lost through the overflow pipe, which had deliberately been blocked off to prevent this from happening. Instead, the steam from the boiling water was blown off into a can that was bolted to the running board and half filled with water. When the engine cooled, the trapped steam would condense and the topped-up water would be sucked back into the radiator.

'If it works properly, without leaking,' Monkey told them, 'you can go the whole life of the truck without ever putting water in after the initial top-up.'

'Pure bleedin' genius,' Taff, a car enthusiast, said in genuine admiration.

'Right, men,' Monkey said, grinning from ear to ear with pleasure at Taff's remark. 'Into your vehicles and let's go.'

The men all piled into their respective Chevrolets and were driven out of the palm-fringed oasis into the vast, barren wastes of the desert. Immediately assailed by the ferocious heat, they were grateful for the wind created by the vehicles' forward movement, even though this also created huge clouds of sand that threatened to choke them. Covering their faces with their *shemaghs*, they could keep the sand out of their mouths and nostrils, but that in turn made breathing difficult. Within minutes they were all sweating profusely and covered in a fine film of sand that stuck like slime to their sweat. Within half an hour most of them felt that they were in hell and some of them were already feeling nauseous.

After only an hour's drive, Sergeant William 'Wild Bill' Monnery ordered all vehicles to stop and the drivers got out to check the tyres, let some air out lest they burst from heat, and make sure that there was no sand in the carburettors. They also checked the petrol, oil and water, adjusted the compasses, and checked all weapons for sand blockage.

The SAS passengers were obliged to do the same and most of them, to their dismay, found that their weapons already had sand in them and had to be cleaned. When it became clear that most of them were unable to clean their weapons properly because of the sand still blowing, the LRDG corporals showed them how to do it blind. A towel was thrown over the weapon resting on the man's lap and the separate components were cleaned and reassembled beneath it. This process, which was frustrating and caused a lot of angry swearing, was repeated time and again until the SAS troopers got it right. And as they were soon to learn, with increasing despair, this tedious procedure was carried out every hour on the dot, greatly lengthening the time of the journey and causing a great deal of exhausting work.

Eventually, when the noon sun was almost directly overhead and the heat was truly ferocious, they stopped in the middle of what seemed like a boundless, barren wasteland, where they were told they would be making camp for the night. Shelters were raised by tying the top ends of waterproof ponchos to the protuberances of the vehicles and the bottom ends to small stakes in the ground. In some cases, where the men did not like the smell of petrol, they made similar shelters by using three-foot-long sticks as uprights instead of a vehicle's protuberances. In both cases, however, a groundsheet was spread out on the desert floor beneath the triangular poncho tent.

Exhausted already, covered in a fine layer of sweaty sand and burnt by the sun, the men crawled into their shelters with a great deal of relief, hoping to enjoy the shade as they ate a light lunch of sandwiches, known as 'wads', with hot tea and a cigarette.

Their pleasure was short-lived, as they were allowed only a thirty-minute break before being called back out into the blazing heat and informed by Wild Bill Monnery, with his grimly smiling fellow sergeant Lorrimer by his side, that they had to hump their heavy bergens onto their backs, pick up two small weapons – a rifle and a sub-machine-gun – and follow the two of them into the desert to learn navigation.

'So why do we need the bergens and weapons?' Neil Moffatt asked resentfully.

'Because we're simulating a real hike across the desert and that's what you'll be carrying.'

It was murder. They hiked for four hours and

only stopped, about every hour, to learn one of the various methods of desert navigation. After being trained in the proper use of a compass and sextant, they were shown how to make an improvised compass by stroking a sewing needle in one direction against a piece of silk and suspending it in a loop of thread so that it pointed north; by laying the needle on a piece of paper or bark and floating it on water in a cup or mess tin; or by stropping a razor blade against the palm of the hand and, as with the sewing needle, suspending it from a piece of thread to let it point north.

By last light they had learnt that although in the featureless desert maps were fairly useless, they could get a sense of direction from a combination of marked oases and drawn contour lines. Whereas the marked oases gave a specific indication of direction, the contour lines showed changes in height which represented wadis, escarpments, particular areas known for their sand dunes, and the difference between convex and concave slopes, the latter being impossible to climb and so best avoided. They also learnt how to find local magnetic variations, when not recorded on a map, by pointing their compass at the North Star and noting the difference between the pointer and the indicated north. Lastly, while the sun was still up, they were shown how to ascertain direction by planting a three-foot upright in the desert floor, marking the tip of its shadow with a pebble or stick, marking the tip of the moving shadow fifteen minutes later, and joining the two with a line which would run from east to west, thus revealing north and south as well. This was known as the 'shadow stick method'.

Once darkness fell, bringing the blessing of cool air, they were made to march even deeper into the desert. There they were taught to navigate by the timing of the rise and fall of the moon, or by the position of certain stars or constellations.

'So,' Wild Bill asked at the end of the final lesson, when the SAS men were unmistakably exhausted, 'did you understand all that?' Eager to return to base and get some sleep, the troopers either said 'Yes!' or nodded affirmatively. 'Good,' Wild Bill said, climbing up into his Chevrolet, just as the other LRDG men, along with that other experienced desert hand, Sergeant Lorrimer, were doing the same. 'If that's the case, let's see you prove it by making your own way back to the camp. Goodbye and good luck!'

Temporarily shocked speechless, the SAS troopers just stood there as the LRDG trucks roared off, churning up great clouds of sand, and eventually disappeared into the darkness, letting the eerie silence of the desert settle around the men.

'Jesus!' Frankie said, almost whispering, glancing about him at the vast, moonlit wilderness. 'This is pretty scary.'

'I'm not scared, I'm exhausted,' Neil said. 'I don't think I can walk a step.'

Taff studied the stars, recalled what he had been taught, then pointed towards the invisible horizon with his index finger. 'That way, lads. Let's go.'

They began the long hike back to the camp.

Surprisingly, they all made it back. Some had fallen behind, others had broken away from the main group and become temporarily lost, but all of them made it back somehow, albeit in the early hours of the morning and in a state of utter exhaustion.

Falling straight onto the groundsheets under their poncho covers, they attempted to sleep, but found it almost impossible. Some were too exhausted to sleep, others dozed fitfully, and all were tormented by a combination of the freezing cold and the usual swarms of fat black flies, mosquitoes and midges, which buzzed and whined constantly in their ears, seemingly oblivious to the cold. Curses exploded up and down the separate tents as the men tossed and turned and, in some instances, gave up altogether, lighting cigarettes and talking instead.

'Cor blimey,' Jimbo said to Frankie, lying next to him, 'I don't mind being in the Army, doing my bit, but this place is bloody ridiculous. For the first time since I've been away, I've been thinking of home.'

'Wapping, wasn't it?' Frankie asked.

'S'right. Good old Wapping. I was there when it took the brunt of the Blitz, but I didn't mind that. When the air-raid sirens wailed, we didn't go to the bomb shelters; we just locked the doors of the pub and sat out the bombing. Buildings ablaze all around us and the ARP and Fire Brigade at work, but we knocked back the mild and bitter and sang our songs until it was all over. They're a good lot in Wapping.'

'What about the missus?'

'What about her?'

'She all right?'

'Not bad, I suppose. I mean, I could've done worse. She kept the house clean and looked after the kids. A decent girl, really. But I joined up before the war started, so I didn't see her that much.'

'That's why you're still married.'

They both chuckled at that, inhaled and blew clouds of smoke. Allied aircraft were passing overhead, very high in the sky. When they were gone, there was silence.

'You were born in London?' Frankie asked.

'Course. Right there in Wapping. Lived there all me life, worked me old man's fruit cart, first Brewer Street, then Covent Garden, but eventually joined the TA, then went into the Army. Smart, see? I knew there was a war on the way and that if I joined up, instead of being conscripted, I'd have certain advantages. That's why I'm now a corporal and you're a private, you poor bleedin' conscript. I joined up the day England beat the Aussies at the Oval and Len Hutton had an innings of 364. I'll never forget that.'

Frankie grinned and had another drag on his cigarette. 'Don't like cricket m'self,' he said. 'I like a bit of football. I follow Arsenal 'cause that's near where I live. They have some good matches there.'

'Bleedin' Paddy Town over there. That's Finsbury Park, ain't it? All them bloody Paddies livin' off the bleedin' dole. Should send 'em back on the boat.'

'Good place, Finsbury Park. Lively. Know what I mean? The Paddies enjoy a good time in the pub, plenty of chat, and are a generous lot. There's lots of Paddies in my street and they're a good bunch. My Mum and Dad swear by them.'

'You live with your Mum and Dad?'

'Never left home,' Frankie said. 'We have a nice three-storey house in Stroud Green Road. The tube's only five minutes' walk and the buses go right past us.' Frankie's father was a train driver on the London and North-Eastern Line, between London and Newcastle, while his mother looked after the house and enjoyed her neighbours' company. 'Now there's air-raid shelters up the side streets and black-out curtains all over the show. My girlfriend's keen on black-out curtains. It makes her feel safe.'

'You mean . . .?'

'You've got it. We know we're not being watched when we do it.'

In fact, like most of his mates Frankie lied about his girlfriend Pam and only did 'it' with her in his dreams. Of course he had groped her a lot, sucked her tits, but that was about as far as he had got in the eighteen months that he had known her. She was a respectable girl from Crouch End, up the hill, which put her a cut above him – or so she thought. She wanted respect, so she had told him, and that could only mean marriage. Frankie, who had a good life at home, and was spoilt by both of his parents and two doting older sisters, had his doubts about leaving home for marriage. A man could make a mistake that way.

'Funny, ain't it?' he said.

'What?'

'The way we think about London,' Frankie went on, 'about it being divided up into areas with different classes of people, that's the way people think of the whole country. Divided between north and south, I mean. You take Neil there, and Taff Clayton – they think they're real folk up in the north while we're artificial.'

'Taff Clayton's a Welshman.'

'But he thinks the same way. The Welsh and the Scots, they think just like the northerners. They think they're better – more real and genuine – than we are in the south. It's a queer thing, ain't it?'

'I wouldn't give the time of day to the north of England,' Jimbo replied. 'Nor to Scotland or Wales. A right worthless shower they are.'

'Neil and Taff are all right,' Frankie said, suddenly feeling sentimental and generous towards his mates.

'They're a pair of piss-heads,' Jimbo replied. 'They don't know the real world.'

Frankie sighed. 'Yeah, I suppose you're right.'

Jimbo mumbled something else and then started snoring. Frankie swatted the flies away and lit up another Senior Service. He could not sleep to save his life; he was just too tired.

The men were up at first light the second day, some having slept only a couple of hours, some none at all, to swallow a quick breakfast of wads and hot tea, desperately trying to protect both from the swarms of bloated black flies and mosquitoes that had driven most of them mad throughout the night.

After breakfast and a clean-up, with their mess kit put away, they had their final shit in that place and then poured petrol over the temporary latrines, lit it and burned everything. It seemed an odd thing to do in the middle of the desert, but no one thought to question it – or indeed had time to do so – as they were then obliged to hurriedly dismantle their shelters, roll and pack their groundsheets and ponchos, remove all signs of the camp, and load their gear in preparation for another drive into the desert.

Before setting off, however, they gathered around their LRDG instructors, in the already fierce heat of the morning, to receive lessons in how to maximize the use of their precious water. The first method was to clean their teeth, spit the tiny amount of water in their mouth out into a container, use that to shave with, then put it into the radiator of their vehicle. Monkey Madson then showed them how to make an improvised filtering system out of stacked four-gallon petrol cans, using a layer of sand and small stones in the top can, pouring the dirty water onto it, and letting it drip through to the lower can, when it could be recycled.

'You can also use one of these instead of the layer of sand and stones,' Monkey said, removing the filter from a captured Italian gas mask and placing it over the opening in the top can. 'So, when you've picked up your meagre water-bottle ration, you clean your teeth, swill your gob out with the water, then spit the water into the filter to run back into the can.'

'I feel ill already!' Neil said.

'Then,' Monkey continued enthusiastically, 'when you've got half a can of water, you wash your face in it and pour it back into the top can to be filtered and used again. You can even wash your socks in it, then, as before, pour the dirty water back into the can to be filtered and ...'

'Fucking great,' Jimbo said. 'You clean your teeth with it, wash yourself with it, wash your socks and shitty underpants in it ... and drink it as well. I don't think I'm hearing right.'

'You heard right,' Monkey told him. 'It's a

continuous recycling process and you better get used to it. Mind you, most of us don't drink the water as such; we have it as a brew-up. That way you can swallow it.'

To the amusement of the others, Taff rammed his fingers down his throat and pretended to choke and die.

'We're moving out!' Wild Bill Monnery bawled, interrupting Taff's act. 'Get to your vehicles!'

This time, when they were driven out into the fierce heat of the wilderness, they were taught to drive the Chevrolets across smooth, hard ground, up and down deep wadis and steep sand dunes, and across a rocky terrain that alternated dangerously with patches of soft sand and gravel – and to fire the weapons fixed to the vehicles while doing so.

When going through soft sand, the vehicles often became bogged down and had to be dug out; the men learnt the hard way just what the sand mats and channels fixed to the vehicles were for. Invariably, the nose of the car would be tipped right forward, the axle buried deep in the sand. Getting it out was dreadfully hard work that would have been impossible without the sand mats and channels. The former were woven mats; the latter were heavy metal channels five feet long that had originally been used in World War One as the roofing for dugouts.

First, the men had to unload all their gear from the vehicle to make it lighter. After laboriously digging and scraping the sand away from the wheels of the trapped vehicle, they pushed the sand mats under the front wheels and the steel sand channels under the rear wheels. When these were firmly in place between the wheels and the soft sand, the vehicle, with its engine running in low gear, could then be pushed forward onto a succession of other sand mats and channels until it was back on harder ground.

It was a sweaty, back-breaking, exhausting business that had to be done at least every couple of hours.

'I'll never joke about the LRDG again,' Jimbo said breathlessly to Frankie, after both of them had helped rescue their Chevrolet. 'These blokes earn their pennies!'

After a full day of this kind of activity in the relentless heat of the barren plains, the men were about ready to collapse when ordered to stop and make up a camp for their second night in the desert. However, once they had put up their poncho shelters, where they had hoped to relax while waiting for the cook to prepare the evening meal, they were dragged out by Wild Bill to be instructed in the art of desert cooking.

This lesson was given by Corporal Tod 'The Toad' Harrington, a great beast of a man who drove them crazy with hunger when, instead of cooking for them, he arrived in their midst with a portable soldering kit and took two hours showing them how to make their own cooker out of a large biscuit tin and a small cheese tin. After cutting the latter in two, he poured sand and petrol into one half, to be used as fuel. He then cut holes in two sides of the biscuit tin, put a funnel through the middle, welding it to the sides of the holes, then surrounded it with a water jacket that contained a gallon of water and could be brought to the boil in three minutes when placed over the burning petrol in the cheese tin.

'Any questions?' he asked the men sitting around him in the sand, most of them nearly demented with exhaustion and hunger.

'Yeah,' Jimbo said. 'When do we eat?'

Grinning maliciously, the Toad picked up the hard biscuits he had removed from the biscuit tin before turning it into a cooker, placed them on a large stone, then proceeded to pulverize them with the handle of his handgun. When they were completely crushed, he scraped the crumbs into the unused other half of the cheese tin, added condensed milk, jam, sugar and hot water from the modified biscuit tin, then stuck a spoon in it and handed it to Jimbo.

'*Voilà!*' the Toad exclaimed in a tone that suggested whisky had ruined his vocal cords.

Jimbo looked down in disgust at the steaming mess in the cheese tin. 'What the fuck is it?'

'Porridge!' the Toad explained proudly.

'Vomit, vomit!' Taff gurgled, again sticking his fingers down his throat.

Nevertheless, they were fed that night, not with the Toad's porridge, but with his bully beef, tinned M and V, dehydrated potatoes, herrings in tomato and some noodles obviously rifled from the Italians.

'It's an international cuisine,' the Toad explained, 'so I want no complaints.'

'We're too busy gagging to complain,' Frankie replied, 'so you've no need to worry about that.'

Attempting to sleep out in the open that night, on the cold groundsheets under their poncho tents, but otherwise exposed to the freezing cold and the relentless flies, mosquitoes and midges, which appeared able to defy the cold, Taff and Neil tossed and turned, moaned and groaned, then gave up and lit cigarettes – Taff a Woodbine, Neil a Players – and tried to pass the time with conversation.

'Amazing, isn't it?' Neil said, his words following a cloud of smoke out of his trembling lips. 'Here we are, two working-class lads who otherwise probably would never have left their home towns, in the middle of the bleeding North African desert, looking up at the stars.'

'Very poetic,' Taff said. 'I've got a lump in my throat already.'

'No, seriously, I mean it. I mean, here we are, just two common lads, and now we're members of the toughest regiment in the British Army, fighting in a desert in North Africa. It really makes you think, doesn't it?'

'How the bleedin' 'ell did *you* get in the Army?' Taff asked him, not being in the mood for philosophy.

'I was a weekend soldier,' Neil replied solemnly. 'Territorial Army. I volunteered in my local drill hall, in Blackburn. On 11 April 1939 – the day Glasgow banned darts in pubs as too dangerous. That's how I'll always remember it. I mean, what kind of people would stoop to that? Bleeding mad, those Scots are.'

Taff recalled the first air-raid shelters, the evacuation of the children from the cities, the eerie silence when the kids had left; then the beginning of the war, the first air-raids, the pounding ack-ack guns and exploding flak, the German bombers and Spitfires, the blazing, crumbling buildings of bombed cities. He thought of all that and wondered how on earth Neil could only remember the day he had volunteered to fight as the day darts were banned from Glaswegian pubs. You wouldn't credit it, would you?

'Aye, right,' he said, getting back to mad Scots. 'We should send them all to Blackburn, where they'd seem perfectly sane.'

'Ha, ha,' Neil said. 'How did *you* get in the Army? Volunteered as well, did you?'

'Are you bloody mad? You think I've got a hole in *my* head? I'd rather be down in the coal mines of Aberfan – that's where I lived and worked, mate – than takin' a lot of bloody shite from English Army thickheads. I didn't *volunteer*, mate. I was bloody conscripted. I tried sayin' I was doin' a job that was in the national interest, but the bastards replied that bein' single I could serve better elsewhere. They then put me on the bus with all the others and drove me away from the village. Booted me into boot camp, then into the Welsh Guards. So, here I am, mate.'

'Not only in L Detachment, SAS, but now a

corporal to boot. If you hate the Army so much, how did you manage that?'

Taff puffed a cloud of smoke while tapping his temple with his forefinger and giving Neil the wink. 'No screws lost here, mate. I made the best of a bad thing. I was good at soldiering, see? I mean, the mines toughened me up. So when I saw that I was good, I thought what the hell, and decided to milk it for all it was worth by tryin' to get a quick promotion. Worked my fanny off, ended up in Tripoli, and was shipped on leave to Alexandria just before Jerry surrounded Tobruk. Then, while still on leave, I read Captain Stirling's memo about that meeting in Geneifa and thought there might be something in it for me. When I heard him talkin' I figured he might be a man goin' places, so I decided to volunteer to go with him. Now, here I am, in the middle of the North African desert, gazing up at the stars. I feel a right bleedin' Charlie!'

He stubbed his cigarette out, lit another, and blew a couple of smoke rings. One of them ringed the pale moon and then dissolved into it.

'You're not a Charlie,' Neil told him. 'You're a good soldier, Taff'. I mean, you come from Wales and the Welsh are like northerners: they're real folk, they endure, they have qualities you don't find in the south. Know what I mean, Taff?'

'The bloody English!' Taff exclaimed. 'I mean those bastards from the south. I don't mean the northerners like you – they're a good-hearted lot – but them Londoners and the like, they all have airs and graces, even if they come from the working class.'

'Jimbo's all right.'

'I'll give you that. He's not bad. But that Frankie from Finsbury Park, he thinks he's cock o' the walk.'

'It's being born in the south, being a Londoner, that makes him that way. He can't help it.'

'They'd blunt his tongue in Aberfan,' Taff replied, 'if he wagged it as much as he does with us. Still, he's all right, I reckon.'

'A good soldier,' Neil said.

'That's why he's here,' Taff said. 'As Jimbo said, L Detachment is the cream de la cream and that makes us somethin' special, see?'

Receiving no response, he glanced to the side and saw the cigarette fall from Neil's fingers and drop into the drifting sand. It smouldered there for a minute, the smoke curling upwards, spiralling in front of Neil's closed eyes before vaporizing. By the time it had gone out, Neil had started snoring.

'Silly sod!' Taff whispered, then he too closed his weary eyes and was soon fast asleep.

The third day was taken up with desert survival, including tactics for avoiding dehydration, sunstroke and sunburn; locating and using artesian wells; hunting desert gazelles for food; the correct disposal of garbage and human waste; desert camouflage and the digging of shallow 'scrapes' and other lying-up positions; treatment of the bites of poisonous spiders, scorpions and snakes, or illness caused by lice, mites, flies and mosquitoes; using condoms to keep dust out of weapons; constructing a desert still to produce drinkable water from urine; and avoiding drowning when caught in a wadi during a flash flood.

'Drowning in the desert!' Frankie laughed. 'You wouldn't credit it, would you?'

Though close to serious exhaustion, he was actually in a good mood because he and the others had just about survived the long day and were scheduled to return to Jalo Oasis that evening, when they could have a decent meal in the mess tent, get drunk in their own tents, and have a desperately needed sleep on a real camp-bed.

For that very reason he almost went into a state

of shock when told by Wild Bill – while Sergeant Lorrimer smiled sadistically right there beside him – that they would indeed be returning that evening – but they had to do it on foot, navigating in the darkness by themselves.

'That should get you back to the oasis by first light,' Wild Bill said. 'Always assuming, of course, that you don't get lost.'

Frankie was not the only soldier who almost gave up there and then, but in the event neither he nor any of the other SAS troopers did. Encouraged by those temporarily less exhausted, they began the long march. They managed to keep going and even repaid a debt by encouraging those who had encouraged them and who, suddenly exhausted, were themselves about to give up. All in all, then, they learned to lean on one another until, just before first light, they all finally made it back. They were a sorry sight to behold, but their pride was obvious.

Impressed, Sergeant Lorrimer let them all have a fry-up washed down with cold beer, followed by a shower and a sleep that lasted till noon.

When they were up dressed, they were called to Stirling's tent, where they were told by the tall, aristocratic captain that the rest of the day was free, but that the following morning they would begin their preparations for the raids against the German airfields.

'Ready, willing and able,' Jimbo said.

He spoke for every one of them.

9

Pleased with the report from Sergeant Monnery on the successful training of the SAS troopers in the desert, Captain Stirling left the Jalo Oasis after dawn on Sunday 8 December, a couple of days earlier than originally planned, to raid the airfield at Sirte.

'I'm anxious to get on with it,' he explained to Brigadier Reid, 'because we could be recalled to Cairo any time. There are still too many officers on the GHQ staff who prefer more orthodox methods of warfare and resent what we're doing out here. They tend to think that L Detachment – and the LRDG as well – are using the guerrilla-warfare tactics of which they so strongly disapprove. In fact, when last I was in Cairo one of those bloody fools told me that this was an ungentlemanly way to fight – one not suited to the forces of the British Empire. That particular officer may be a pompous idiot, but he has many friends.'

'I agree,' Reid said as they shared a cup of tea in his big tent near one of the palm-fringed pools of the oasis. Through the open flaps, between the tent and the pool, the trucks of the first patrol, camouflaged pink and green to blend in with the desert, were gathered together, surrounded by the LRDG and SAS men preparing to leave. 'You'd better get out of here before they stop you – and nothing's lost if you're early. Gives you time for a little mistake or two. Time to change your plans if necessary. Are all the patrols leaving today?'

'No. I want to make the maximum use of surprise, so Captain Lewes will be attacking Agheila airfield the same night as the other patrols hit Sirte.'

'That's only half the distance that you have to travel.'

'Exactly. So although we're attacking the same night, Lewes won't be setting out with S Patrol until two days after I leave.'

'Who's taking you, David?'

'S1 Patrol.

'Commanded by Captain Gus Halliman – a good man.'

'Indeed.' Stirling glanced back over his shoulder

and saw that the last of the men had taken his place in his Chevrolet. 'They're all set to leave,' Stirling said. 'I'd best be going.' He stood up and offered his hand to the brigadier. The two men shook hands.

'Good luck and God speed,' Reid said warmly.

'Thank you, sir,' Stirling replied, then left the tent, climbed into his designated Chevrolet lorry, and nodded to Captain Halliman, indicating that they could now start the journey. Halliman nodded back, then raised and lowered his right hand. The lorries all roared into life simultaneously, then moved out of the oasis, churning up billowing clouds of sand in their wake. They soon reached the vast open plains of the desert where, with the force of a hammer, the sun's blazing heat hit them.

Halliman, a big-boned, fair-haired Englishman, led his mainly Rhodesian drivers with the confidence of a man who knew the desert well. In fact, he had served in the Royal Tank Corps before joining the LRDG, but his experience with the latter was considerable and now he was one of their best men. He rode in the leading truck with his navigator, Mike Sadler, another Rhodesian.

Stirling and Captain 'Paddy' Callaghan were in the second truck with their nine SAS troopers perched all around them where they could get a footing on the piles of gear. Indeed, each of the seven trucks was close to being overloaded with petrol, water-cans, blankets, camouflage nets, weapons, ammunition, and the seventeen other men of the LRDG. However, the LRDG put great faith in the reinforced springs of their vehicles and so drove on into the dazzling light of the desert with calm confidence.

'I hope these Rhodesian bastards know where they're going,' Jimbo said, not as confident as the drivers appeared to be. 'I don't want to be lost in this bleedin' desert.'

'I think we're in safe hands,' Frankie told him. 'They seem pretty capable.'

'I'll believe it when I see it, my old mate. For now, I'm keeping a tight arse.'

'I'll stop holding my nose then.'

The LRDG men worked to a routine that was automatically followed by the SAS troopers. As the day warmed up, they shed the sheepskin jackets that kept out the chill of the early hours. By 1000 hours the sun was well up in the sky, at over 20 degrees, throwing a sharp shadow from the needle of the sun compass so bright that it started to hurt the men's eyes. An hour later the blasts of warm air on the ridge tops had forced the gunners perched high on each lorry to discard most of their clothes. By noon, with the sun almost directly above them and the desert plain had taken on a stark, white lunar quality, the vehicles were halted in the shadow of a steep wadi side where they would not be seen by overflying enemy aircraft.

'Thank Christ for that,' Jimbo said as Mike Sadler took a fix on the sun through the smoked glass of his theodolite, the radio operator contacted base for any fresh orders, and the rest of the men lay under the shade of a tarpaulin stretched between two trucks. 'You could have fried a bloody egg on my head, it was getting so hot.'

'I feel like gagging in this heat,' Frankie replied, 'it dries my throat out so.'

'Hey, Taff!' Jimbo called out to the Welshman, who was sitting in the shade of his own truck, smoking. 'Is that dark stain around your crutch sweat or have you just been tugging it off again?'

Taff stared steadily, sardonically, at Jimbo, then thoughtfully blew a couple of smoke rings and watched them dissolving. 'At least I've got something to tug,' he said. 'I have my doubts about you, lad.'

Jimbo grinned. He always enjoyed a good comeback. 'I'm told the Welsh are very good at singing when they reach the crescendo.'

'We always climax well,' Taff responded, 'and leave the audience gasping.'

'With horror, no doubt.'

'On your feet!' Sergeant Lorrimer roared. 'Move it! Let's go!'

'He can sing even better than you,' Jimbo said to Taff, as they climbed to their feet with the others.

'Right,' Taff said. 'A heavenly choir. It reverberates endlessly. Well, here we go again.'

By early afternoon they had left Jalo well behind them and were heading for El Agheila, across the perfectly smooth, hard sand of a vast landscape, with the sheer cliffs of the upland plateaux visible beyond the heat haze in the north and alluvial sand dunes, awesomely beautiful, rising and falling to the west. For most of the afternoon the heat was truly appalling, felt particularly on the head even through the black woollen *agal* and *shemagh*, but it cooled to more bearable levels in the late afternoon, when Halliman started looking out for a place to laager before last light. By the time he had found a suitable spot, again in a shaded wadi, the patrol had travelled over 90 miles from Jalo. Luckily, the day had been without incident other than the usual punctures, trucks bogged down in soft sand and the minor repairs required after motoring over grit, sand and rock. They had not seen any sign of the enemy; nor had they caught a glimpse of a single Arab.

'This place is as empty as the far side of the moon,' Callaghan said to Stirling. 'We're the only ones here.'

'I wouldn't bet on that,' Halliman said, climbing down from the lorry. 'Don't relax for a second.'

When the vehicles laagered, they parked across the wind. Each driver then pinned the folded tarpaulin by two wheels on the lee side, with the upper half forming a windbreak and the lower a groundsheet. Before resting, however, the LRDG drivers had to check their day's petrol consumption and make the usual maintenance checks, including water, oil, tyres and the possible clogging of the carburettor with sand. While the drivers were doing this, the SAS were checking and cleaning their weapons with equal thoroughness, even though they had already tried to protect them from the sand by wrapping them, to the accompaniment of many ribald remarks and howls of laughter, in stretched condoms.

Meanwhile, the cooks had a fire going (which almost certainly would be mistaken for an Arab camp fire by Axis aircraft flying overhead) and water on the boil for a brew of tea. When this was ready, the men drank it gratefully, smoked a lot of cigarettes, washed themselves as best they could, trying to get rid of the blend of sweat and sand, and then tucked in enthusiastically to the 'international cuisine' dreamt up by the immense Corporal Harrington. It was some kind of bully-beef curry and it wasn't half bad.

Afterwards the men stretched out under the trucks and tried to sleep as best they could, given that the night was bitterly cold and that the buzzing flies and whining mosquitoes were oblivious to it. You could hardly call it a restful night.

The following morning Captain Stirling received a signal from Jalo stating that the main battle was static, with Rommel at Gazala and the Eighth Army reorganizing for a further advance. Now even more confident that they were doing the right thing, he passed the news on to Halliman, who, over the next two days, moved the patrol steadily north-westwards towards Sirte.

Just before the midday halt on the third day, approximately 65 miles south of Sirte, an Italian Gibli fighter plane, lightly armed but highly manoeuvrable, appeared seemingly out of nowhere, its wings glinting like silver in the clear blue sky.

It banked to begin its attack descent.

'Damn!' Stirling exclaimed. 'That blighter could radio our position back to his HQ.'

'He could also blow us to Kingdom Come,' Halliman replied, glancing back at the rest of his column, which was crossing a rocky stretch of desert at a mere 6 mph with no shelter in sight. 'That's all *I* need to know.' He turned to his black-bearded Rhodesian gunner and snapped, 'Open fire!'

The Boyes anti-tank rifle roared into life, firing a hail of bullets and tracer at the Gibli as it barrelled down out of the azure sky, its own machine-guns hammering as it dived and making the sand spit in long, jagged lines that snaked towards the slow-moving vehicles. The other LRDG gunners also opened fire, but failed to hit the plane as it dropped its two bombs. It levelled out, roared very low overhead and ascended again, just as the bombs exploded with a deafening roar.

Sand and soil erupted in mushrooming smoke to the east of the column, showering the men as it rained back down again. The Italian plane flew off and disappeared into the heat haze as the exploded sand and soil settled, some of it still smouldering, and the black smoke trailed away, revealing two enormous charred holes in the desert plain's bleached white surface, mere

156

yards from the trucks, which continued to move forward, untouched.

'Close one,' Stirling said.

'We didn't hit that bastard,' Halliman reminded the others, 'and he's flown back to his base. Before very long, his friends will come back to look for us. We'd better go into hiding.' He turned around in the lorry and raised his right hand, indicating 'Stop'. Then, when the other drivers had come to a halt, he swung the same hand out from the hip and back in again, indicating 'Follow me'. He then told his Rhodesian driver to backtrack to where he had seen a patch of scrub that could be the basis for a camouflaged position. When they arrived there and Halliman could survey the area properly, he realized that there was not enough scrub to camouflage the vehicles but just enough, in combination with the camouflage nets, to give decent cover.

Turning to Wild Bill Monnery, he said: 'Sergeant, tell the men to form a laager inside this area of scrub and then fling their cam nets over the vehicles and move well clear of them. Also, get some of the men to hike out to where we were and erase all signs of our tracks from our main route to here. There's no point in trying to fight off an air attack, as any machine-gun fire will only draw attention to the vehicles hidden under the netting. So tell the men to simply lie low until the enemy planes have come and gone. Then we'll move on.'

When Monnery conveyed Halliman's orders to the men, they did as they were told, the drivers forming a tight laager close to the scrub, other men covering the trucks with camouflage nets, and some of them hiking back out to where they had been attacked, to erase the tracks of the trucks by brushing the sand over them as they made their way back to the laager.

With their woven shreds of desert-coloured hessian, the nets blended perfectly with the surrounding shrub, making the lorries practically invisible from the air. The vehicles' tracks, though trailing back across the desert where the column had come from, stopped dead where the column had been attacked. From the air it would now be difficult to know where the column had gone.

Still in their parked vehicles, almost suffocating under the heavy camouflage nets, the men waited for the Italian aircraft to arrive. No one spoke. The tension was contagious. Eventually, after what seemed like hours, but was in fact forty minutes, three Italian bombers flew overhead, searching for the tracks of the vehicles. They found only the tracks well away from the patch of scrub and turned back to strafe that area and also drop a number of small bombs. The explosions, when they came, were both noisy and spectacular, great mushrooms of sand, soil and smoke, but they destroyed nothing more than the desert's formerly unblemished surface.

'My compliments,' Stirling whispered to Halliman. 'That was a good idea.'

Halliman just grinned.

Once the clouds of sand and dust had settled, the Italian aircraft departed and the men picked themselves up and went back to their vehicles. No one was hurt and no damage had been done – not even a tyre punctured – so the men settled down to a lunch of wads and tinned fruit. The latter, in particular, drove the flies and mosquitoes into a frenzy of buzzing and whining.

'We'll move off again at 1400 hours,' Halliman told Stirling and Paddy Callaghan as they had their meagre lunch in the shade of the former's Chevrolet. 'We intend dropping you and your men off at a point about three miles from Sirte and approximately the same distance from the coast road – far closer to Axis traffic than we'd normally take vehicles when on reconnaissance. We should be there by midnight.'

'You've done a damned good job so far,' Paddy Callaghan said. 'Very impressive. I must say.'

'What we do, we do well,' Halliman replied. 'I think that's something you understand.'

'Absolutely!' Stirling affirmed.

Halliman grinned. 'I knew you'd say that. Now it's time to move on.'

The following five hours were uneventful, other than for the expected difficulties, all of which, combined, doubled the time the same journey would have taken on a decent road and trebled the workload of the already exhausted men.

To add to their frustration, a second Italian fighter plane spotted them just before last light, when they only had 40 miles to go. It swept down unexpectedly, making a dreadful din, to rake the convoy with its machine-guns, then drop its two little bombs. As before, the explosions were catastrophic but well off the mark, creating a spectacle of mushrooming sand, dust and smoke, but doing no damage to the column. Having run out of ammunition, the pilot eventually flew away.

'Charming people, the Italians,' Stirling said, 'but obviously as blind as bats.'

'That's why you're charmed by them,' Callaghan told him. 'You think the Eyeties are harmless.'

The column pressed on, now closed up in convoy

formation, no longer spread out as a precaution against an air attack.

'No point,' Halliman explained. 'We're practically there.'

They covered the last 20 miles without using their headlights, which made for a bumpy, dangerous ride. Eventually, as most of them suspected would happen, a bad combination of unseen pothole and soft sand led to another vehicle, the last in the convoy, being bogged down only 1600 yards from the DZ selected by Halliman.

It was clear that it would take a long time to dig out the lorry.

'Damn!' Stirling exploded as a bunch of his men hurried to rescue the bogged-down vehicle with sand mats and steel channels. 'This could cause complications.'

'Damned right, it could,' Callaghan replied. 'It could take hours to dig out the bloody thing.'

'And the pilot of that last Gibli,' Halliman added, 'is bound to alert his fellow Eyeties to our presence here. A change of plan is called for.'

Standing upright in the rear of the Chevrolet, glancing at the darkening desert plain all around him, clearly boiling up with frustration, Stirling lit a consoling cigarette, blew a cloud of smoke, then nodded, as if at a ghost, and finally spoke.

'Right!' He turned to Callaghan. 'If we fail to hit Sirte, we'll attack at least one other airfield and the way to do that is to break up. There's a new airfield at Tamit, about 30 miles west of here, and I want you, Paddy, to take eight men and hit it.'

'Right, boss.'

'Meanwhile, Sergeant Lorrimer and I will take a patrol on foot to raid Sirte.'

'Sounds good to me, boss.'

Stirling checked his watch, then looked up again. 'We'll both plan to set off our charges at 2300 hours tomorrow night. When that's done, Sergeant Lorrimer and I will rendezvous with Captain Halliman back here. The other six lorries – three for each party – will pick up the rest of the raiders in the early hours of the next morning, Friday, and travel independently to the desert RV.' He turned to Halliman. 'Is this feasible?'

Halliman shrugged. 'Who dares wins,' he said.

10

Before the two groups could separate, Corporal Mike Sadler, the LRDG navigator who had been checking their position with a combination of map reading and eyeball recce, returned to Halliman's truck to say that they were far closer to the coast road than he had expected.

'It's lucky we didn't go a further 1600 yards to the north,' he said, 'because there the road bends southwards in a way that isn't shown on this bloody map.'

'What does that mean?' Stirling asked.

'It means we're practically on the perimeter of the Sirte airfield,' Halliman said. 'Practically in the lap of the Germans. It means they could be all around us already and we'd better be careful.'

Even as he was speaking, he thought he heard a distant sound, so he used a hand signal – still just about visible in the evening's dying light – to tell the other drivers to switch off their engines. When they did so, the distant sounds became clearer. First they heard barely distinguishable voices, then the growling of a road-patrol vehicle gathering speed as it moved off.

'That confirms it,' Halliman said. 'Those Gibli pilots have reported our presence in the area and Jerry's now on the alert for a raid against the traffic going along that sea road.'

'It's a Jerry MSR,' Sergeant Lorrimer reminded them, 'so they're bound to be doubly concerned.'

'Then we'd better get started,' Stirling said. 'Get this over and done with before they launch a full-scale search.' He turned to Lorrimer. 'I don't want any tell-tale footprints showing that we separated from the main patrol and headed for Sirte, so let's get ready to jump off a good distance from here, where Jerry's not likely to look for us. Let's get on the running board.'

'Right, boss.' Even as Sadler turned on the ignition and moved off, Lorrimer was clambering over the side to stand on the narrow running board and cling to the door. Because he was carrying a bag of Lewes bombs and fuses, as well as his heavy rucksack, this was more precarious for him than it was for Stirling. As the Chevrolet picked up speed, followed by the others, Stirling did the same at the other side of the vehicle, hanging on precariously and being dragged down by his rucksack while also being whipped by the snapping slipstream.

When the lorry was a good half mile from where the patrol had stopped, still travelling at a mere 15 mph and heading west for the new airfield at Tamit, Stirling shouted, 'Now!' He then threw his carefully wrapped Sten gun to the ground and jumped off the running board.

His parachute training stood him in good stead. Deliberately bending his legs when his feet touched the ground, he let his body relax, tried not to resist the impact, and rolled over a few times, choking in the dust created by his fall, but otherwise unharmed. When he picked himself up, resting there on his knees, he saw Lorrimer doing the same a few yards away. As the sergeant clambered to his feet, brushing the dust off his clothing, he was wearing a big, cheesy grin.

'I'm getting too old for this,' he said, 'but that made me feel like a schoolboy.'

'Me, too,' Stirling said. Looking west, he saw the last of the trucks of S1 patrol, already obscured by dust boiling up in their wake, then eventually disappearing into the darkness.

'Best of luck,' he murmured, then he and Lorrimer looked around for their weapons and the bag of

Lewes bombs. After finding them, they removed the padded wrapping from the weapons and cleaned them thoroughly. This done, Lorrimer picked up the bag of Lewes bombs and fuses, then nodded at Stirling. 'Let's go,' said the latter.

They hiked side by side through the growing darkness, being careful to stay low and listening intently for the sounds of German patrols. The desert plain was hard, a pale white in the moonlit darkness, its flat surface running out to an escarpment overlooking the Mediterranean. It was covered with a fine film of dust, stirred by the wind blowing in from the sea and constantly drifting.

Suddenly, coming up over a low ridge, they saw a group of Italian soldiers marching along in file formation on routine patrol. Throwing themselves to the ground, they waited for the patrol to pass, a mere 15 yards away. Climbing to their feet again, the two SAS men hurried off in the opposite direction, heading away from the escarpment overlooking the sea, down the northern slope, towards the Sirte airfield.

Being much closer to the airfield than they had expected, practically on its perimeter, they soon found themselves making their way between its outer buildings which, to their surprise, were neither fenced in nor guarded. Once past the buildings, they came to the dispersal area, again without hindrance, where they saw a row of unguarded Axis aircraft.

'Italian Capronis,' Lorrimer whispered.

'Very nice, too,' Stirling said. 'Just waiting for a necklace of Lewes bombs and a baptism of fire and smoke.'

'They're certainly tempting,' Lorrimer whispered. 'Why not do it right now?'

'Because by blowing them up now we'd alert them to what we're up to and jeopardize S1's chance of success at Tamit.'

'So what do we do in the meantime?'

'We recce the airfield and plan tomorrow's raid, then we get the hell out of here and find a safe hide.'

'Sounds fair enough to me, boss.'

After counting the aircraft – there were thirty in all – they moved on, circling the airfield and taking note of anything that might help them when they returned as raiders. They saw the odd German guard here and there, wandering lazily to and fro, rifles slung across their shoulders, but they all seemed half asleep and the recce was completed without problems.

Until, on the way back out of the airfield, Stirling

stumbled over the body of an Italian sentry sleeping on the ground.

The man jerked upright automatically, throwing off his blanket. Seeing Stirling and Lorrimer, he yelled a warning, alerting the whole garrison, then reached frantically for his rifle. Stirling kicked the weapon out of the Italian's reach, then he and Lorrimer ran like the wind back the way they had come.

The snap of a firing semi-automatic rifle behind them was followed by the sound of bullets whipping past their heads as the guard they had awakened fired after them. To avoid the rifle fire, they made a sharp left, rolled down a dip in the upward slope, then climbed back to their feet and ran on towards the escarpment. The sentry behind them stopped firing – probably to run back towards the airfield to tell his friends which way the Englishmen had gone.

As Stirling and Lorrimer were hurrying up the slope north of the airfield, sirens started to wail and the guns of the garrison, large and small, began firing out to sea. This noisy barrage soon developed into a full-blown shadow fire-fight as the men in the garrison tried to prevent an imagined assault from the sea or, even worse in their view, from enemy troops advancing inland. The tracers from their anti-aircraft guns looped in beautiful, phosphorescent-purple lines towards the sea, criss-crossing in the dark sky, exploding in black clouds of flak above the water just beyond the escarpment. To the initial clamour of the big guns was added the savage roar of numerous machine-guns and, in one instance of obvious panic, the distant thud of a firing mortar whose shell exploded with a mighty eruption of earth and smoke further down the slope.

Once on the hillside, Stirling and Lorrimer turned east and zigzagged along the edge of the escarpment, under an umbrella of tracer and exploding flak, until they were well away from where the guard would have reckoned them to be. Eventually, feeling safer, they crawled into a patch of bushes, carefully covered themselves with foliage, and watched the rest of the spectacular, colourful fire-fight directed at a non-existent invasion force.

'We really stirred up a hornet's nest there,' Lorrimer said with a grin.

'Yes,' Stirling replied. 'They can't work out if we're attacking by air, sea or land, but they certainly think we've arrived.'

'Do you think they'll come out to find us?'

'No. I think they'll dig in, reinforce their defensive positions and wait for the assault they imagine is about to commence. We're probably fairly safe here.'

'But we're stuck here until tomorrow night.'

'I could do with a good sleep,' Stirling said, 'and that's what I'm going to have.'

He turned on his side, tugged the foliage closer over him, used his rucksack as a pillow and went to sleep quickly. Sighing, thinking he could not possibly sleep in such circumstances, Lorrimer nevertheless did the same, though with his body bent up in a foetal position, wrapped around the bag of Lewes bombs and fuses.

In fact, he too fell asleep within minutes of the end of the firing from the airfield, which left a vast silence only broken by the distant murmur of the sea. The sergeant slept like a log.

When he awoke, just after dawn, Lorrimer found Stirling already awake and scanning the surrounding area with his binoculars. Now, in the early morning light, they found themselves with a good view of the beach dunes to the north, the white houses of Sirte to the west, and, most importantly, their targets at the bottom of the escarpment.

After studying the airfield with some care, Stirling lowered the binoculars and turned to Lorrimer. 'Well,' he said, 'I don't think we can approach the airfield the same way tonight. Every gun in the garrison is probably aimed in that direction. Instead, I suggest we approach by their eastern flank, directly down this hill, sneaking in from the side. Agreed?'

'Agreed.'

Stirling smiled. 'You still look tired, Sergeant.'

'We only slept a couple of hours.'

'That's true enough. My own eyes feel as heavy as lead, so I think I'll rest them again. I strongly recommend you do the same. You'll wake refreshed.'

'I couldn't possibly wake feeling worse, so I'll take your advice.'

Having selected the route by which they would get to the thirty aircraft that night, both men stretched out once more and went back to sleep.

11

They were awoken by the sound of voices and looked up at the same time, seeing only the dazzling azure sky and realizing, from the height of the sun, as well as the appalling heat, that it was still only noon. Not saying a word and trying to move as little as possible, they turned their heads in the direction of the voices and saw two Arab girls, both wearing black veils, stooped over as they toiled with mattocks on one of the few cultivated patches of fertile earth in the surrounding desert.

Stirling and Lorrimer glanced at one another, but again said nothing, fearful that the two girls would hear them. Again studying the girls, they saw that they were intent on their work and had no idea of the presence of two men hiding under the hedges behind them. Unfortunately, there was nothing that Stirling and Lorrimer could do other than wait until the girls had finished their work and left. That could be a long wait.

In fact, it was three hours, during which time Stirling and Lorrimer were forced to lie motionless in their hide, making not a sound, trying not to sneeze, unable even to flex their cramped muscles or relieve their straining bowels. Eventually, however, in the late afternoon, the girls finished work and departed.

'Thank Christ for that,' Stirling said, stretching his long body, flexing his muscles and taking deep breaths to encourage a general relaxation. 'I thought they would never leave.'

'They may have left too late,' Lorrimer replied, pointing at the sky.

Glancing over his shoulder and instantly despairing, Stirling saw that the Italian Capronis were taking off from the airfield and heading inland. They were lifting off two or three at a time and soon an awful lot of them were airborne.

'Oh, damn!' he exclaimed softly. 'I don't believe it!'

'They must be flying to the front,' Lorrimer said, 'to make night attacks against our transports. There go our targets.'

This much was true. As Stirling and Lorrimer looked on in horrified fascination, all the aircraft they had come so far to destroy took off and disappeared beyond the horizon. So agitated was Stirling that he counted them off as they left – 'Fifteen . . . seventeen . . . twenty . . . twenty-three . . .' – mouthing the words silently, in despair, until he had counted a total of thirty and then there were no more.

Every single Caproni spotted on the runway had flown away, leaving nothing to attack. They had gone there for nothing.

Stirling's silent gestures spoke eloquently of his despair. He simply dropped his forehead onto his crooked arm and let it rest there for some time as he took deep, even breaths, trying to soothe his racing heart and subdue his frustration. He remained like that for a long time, as if frozen by dejection, then eventually raised his head again and glanced at the sky, then all around him and finally at Lorrimer.

'I'm think I'm going crazy,' he said. 'I simply cannot accept this.'

'You were always crazy, boss,' Lorrimer replied, 'but you'll just have to accept it. Our targets have gone.'

Lying belly-down, Stirling rested one elbow on the ground, cupped his chin in his hand and gazed first out to sea, then west to the blood-red sun just above the desert's horizon. He stayed in that position for some time, as inscrutable as the Sphinx, then finally sighed, raised himself to his knees and spread his hands as if releasing a trapped bird.

'No use crying over spilt milk,' he said. 'Let's just pray that the others do better than we did. As for us, we might as well go back to the RV and wait for Captain Halliman to pick us up. Not much else to do, is there?'

'Not really,' Lorrimer said, though not without noting the acute disappointment in Stirling's voice. 'It's the luck of the draw, boss.'

After slinging their rucksacks onto their backs, and with Lorrimer again carrying the bag of Lewes bombs and fuses, they headed back to the road in the fading light. Feeling the weight of Stirling's despondency as they made the short hike, Lorrimer was relieved when they reached the road in darkness, just before midnight, and saw flashes and the glow of fires in the far distance, illuminating the western horizon.

'That's Captain Callaghan's group,' he told Stirling, filling up with excitement. 'Tamit's on fire!'

'They've succeeded,' Stirling replied, looking as if he wanted to sprout wings and fly. 'Those flashes are bombs going off. It wasn't *all* wasted, Sergeant!'

Impulsively, they hugged one another, then, getting their senses back, hurried to hide by the side of the road before any Axis traffic came along and saw them.

'Damn it,' Stirling said, 'I can hardly contain myself. We can't just sit here and watch those bombs going off on Tamit airfield. We've got to do *something*.'

Lorrimer glanced up and down the dark road, looking for oncoming Axis traffic. When he saw that nothing was coming, he patted the heavy bag at his feet.

'I have a couple of small land-mines here,' he said, 'so let's plant the buggers.'

'Better than carrying them back,' Stirling responded. 'Yes, damn it, let's do it!'

While Stirling kept watch, Lorrimer unpacked the three small land-mines he had been carrying with the Lewes bombs. After scooping out enough earth to bury them slightly and cover them up again, he spaced them out at equal distances across the road. No traffic came along as he was doing this and soon he was back beside Stirling, hiding in a dip between the road and the desert.

'If Halliman comes along first,' Stirling said, 'let's make sure *he* doesn't drive over the mines.'

'He'll come in off the desert,' Lorrimer said,

'coming right up behind us. We've no need for concern there.'

With nothing else to do but wait, they took the cold food from their rucksacks and ate it while watching the silvery light of the distant explosions in Tamit, which made them feel better. They had finished the food and were just opening their water bottles when an Italian Army oil lorry came along the road from the direction of Sirte, almost certainly heading for the airfield.

Stirling and Lorrimer dropped low, forgetting their thirst, and watched keenly as the huge tanker trundled along the road and ran straight on to the buried land-mines.

The mines went off simultaneously under the front of the vehicle, blowing the surface of the road apart and lifting the driver's cabin right off the ground on a fountain of shattered tarmac with soil and sand spewing up around it. Even as the cabin was rising up and toppling over, the back of the tanker kept moving forward, propelled by its own momentum, and bounced up off the cabin to form a screeching tangle of steel over the confusion of soil and smoke. Then the cabin turned over, smashing sideways onto the road, and the tanker, crashing down onto the cabin, was caught in the heat and force of the exploding land-mines and exploded with even more force, spewing the vivid-yellow fire of blazing oil into the smoke-blackened sky.

The noise was unbelievable, almost palpable in its force, making Stirling and Lorrimer cover their ears, even as the awesome heat from the burning oil swept over them in what seemed like a series of separate, accelerating, scorching blasts. The ground shook beneath them when the tanker crashed back down, bounced once or twice, belching out even more burning oil, then finally settled at the far side of the road in a pool of fire that filled the sky above with billowing black smoke.

In the flames, in that circle of dazzling yellow fire, the steel frame of the tanker, already scorched black, was melting like tar and dripping onto the melting tarmac of the road. The men in the driver's cabin, killed instantly by the blast, were turned into dripping fat and charred, crumbling bone that would, when the flames had died down, be no more than dust.

'Christ!' Lorrimer exclaimed softly. 'I wasn't expecting . . .'

Stirling cut him short by placing his hand on his wrist and gently shaking it. 'A lot of Axis planes will now go short of petrol,' he said. 'We've just done our bit, Sergeant.'

Nevertheless, the fiercely burning vehicle was

bound to draw the attention of the Axis forces in the airfield, so Stirling and Lorrimer were greatly relieved when, at the agreed time, almost to the minute, at 0015 hours, Captain Halliman returned in his LRDG truck to pick them up and drive them back to the desert RV. He glanced at the blazing oil tanker and said, 'What the . . .?'

'Let's go,' Stirling said.

Halliman's driver took them 90 miles across the desert, stopping only to repair the odd puncture, and had them back at the RV by eight the next morning.

'How did it go with Callaghan?' was the first question asked by Stirling when he entered the radio room in Jalo base camp.

12

Captain Callaghan's group had spent an uneventful Thursday before being dropped by the LRDG within striking distance of the Tamit airfield. When the trucks had moved off again, Callaghan glanced around him and saw that he was in the middle of a flat desert plain with no cover whatsoever, other than starlit darkness. The airfield, however, was only a few miles due west and could be seen in the distance, its hangars visible as rectangular blocks darker than the night and framed by the stars. An MSR ran straight through the desert directly to the airfield.

'We're completely exposed out here,' Callaghan told his second-in-command, Jim 'Jimbo' Ashman, 'so let's get there as quickly as humanly possible. Single file. Let's hike it.'

Jimbo raised his right hand with the palm open, to indicate 'Single file', and the men obeyed his silent command, moving out behind him and Callaghan one by one, until they had formed a long, irregular line with Jimbo out front as lead scout, Frankie Turner coming up the rear as Tail-end Charlie, and the rest of the men covering firing arcs to the left and right.

Callaghan, close behind Jimbo, was carrying the bag filled with Lewes bombs and fuses, as well as a Thompson M1928 sub-machine-gun with a 50-round drum magazine. The rest of the men were armed with tommy-guns, Sten guns and Lee-Enfield .303-inch bolt-action rifles. Everyone in the group was also carrying a Browning 9mm High Power handgun holstered at the waist, but otherwise they were travelling light, with no cumbersome rucksacks, or even water bottles, to slow them down. The only sound as they hiked across the flat plain was the clanking of weapons.

Little could be seen in the dark other than the outlying hangars and other buildings of the airfield, which loomed larger and became more detailed as the patrol advanced on them. Surprisingly, there was no fencing around the airstrip and no sentries had so far been seen. Out to the side of the buildings the aircraft were lined up along the runway, a mixture of German Ju-87 Stuka dive-bombers and Italian Capronis, none of them guarded.

They must be pretty sure of themselves, Callaghan thought. Too damned confident for their own good.

About 20 yards from the wooden buildings, he raised his right hand to halt the men, then leaned forward on his left leg and waved the hand in towards his outstretched right leg, signalling that the men behind him should lie belly-down on the ground. When they had done so, Callaghan studied the buildings and noted that a faint line of light was escaping from below the door of one of the wooden huts. Even at this distance, he thought he could hear the murmur of conversation.

Climbing to his feet, he ran forward at the crouch and dropped down again beside Jimbo, who was lying on the ground with his Sten gun aimed at the building.

'You stay here with the men,' Callaghan whispered, 'while I advance and check that building. I think there are soldiers inside.'

'I think you're right,' Jimbo said.

'Take this bag of Lewes bombs. At my signal, or at the first sign of trouble, head straight for those aircraft and destroy them.'

'With you all the way, boss.'

After leaving the bag with Jimbo, Callaghan jumped up and advanced at the crouch until his shadow was touching the line of light beaming out under the door of the long wooden building. The windows were covered in black-out curtains. Stopping at the edge of the line of light, Callaghan heard laughter and a babble of talk from inside. This convinced him that the building was either a mess or the aircrew's briefing hut.

Callaghan, who had been bored for a long time, felt an edge of excitement.

What the hell, he thought. If we try bombing the planes someone's bound to hear us, so I might as well do as much damage here as I possibly can.

He glanced back over his shoulder and saw his men still on the ground. Turning back to the front, he took a deep breath, then kicked the door open and rushed inside.

The light briefly dazzled him. All conversation was stilled. The Germans were gathered around a long table, drinking beer, smoking cigarettes and playing cards or reading. They stared at him, startled, not quite realizing who he was, and were still trying to come to terms with his presence when he opened fire with his tommy-gun.

The noise was shocking in that small space, and made worse by the additional screaming of the men as they died in the hail of bullets, falling out of their chairs or over the table, knocking over bottles and mugs, smashing plates, making ashtrays flip and spin in the air, scattering clouds of grey ash. Others kicked their chairs back and dived to the floor, scrambling under the table, some of them bravely grabbing for their weapons even as the bullets were stitching them.

Callaghan fired in a wide arc, turning from left to right, the roaring weapon jolting his whole body as he backed towards the door. More men shuddered and died. The wounded screamed in pain. Bullets ricocheted off the walls to make a harsh drumming sound that seemed worse when some light-bulbs exploded, plunging the room into semi-darkness.

One of the Germans rolled over, raising his Luger pistol and taking aim, but Callaghan put a short burst into him, shot out the remaining light-bulbs, then backed out through the door as the survivors scrambled frantically in the darkness. As Callaghan stepped outside, some of the Germans in the hut fired their weapons and he heard the bullets whistling past him.

Turning around to face the night, he saw his own men racing across the dark field to get at the Axis aircraft. He raced after them, bullets still hissing by, and only turned around to give the men covering fire when he reached the edge of the airfield. He cut down some of the Germans running out of the building, but others were bunched up behind the windows and firing from there.

'Bugger this for a joke!' Callaghan muttered, determined to blow up some planes himself. 'You men!' he called out to the SAS troopers racing past him. 'I want four of you to stay here and keep those bastards over there occupied. Pour a fusillade of fire through those windows and keep them pinned down.'

'Yes, boss,' Corporal Peterson said, waving three of the troopers over to him. 'Spread out and give covering fire,' he told them. 'Pour it in through those windows.'

The corporal and three privates were already firing a combination of Lee-Enfield .303s and tommy-guns from the kneeling position when Callaghan raced after the other men. He finally caught up with Jimbo, who was kneeling beside a Junkers, distributing Lewes bombs and fuses to the troopers. Some of the men were already racing between the aircraft and lobbing the small bombs up onto their wings as if on a cricket pitch.

'Give me a couple of those,' Callaghan said. 'I've waited a long time for this.'

'Haven't we all?' Jimbo replied, handing Callaghan three of the conveniently small, light bombs. 'The fuses are set for thirty minutes, so don't hang around, boss.'

'I won't,' Callaghan said. Glancing back over his shoulder, he saw that Peterson and his three troopers were still pumping bullets into the hut. Running towards the nearest untouched Italian Caproni to place his first Lewes bomb, Callaghan noticed that when the other men had planted their supply of bombs, they were going back to swell the ranks of Peterson's group and add to the covering fire.

'Good men,' Callaghan whispered as he lobbed his first Lewes bomb up onto the wing of the Caproni. When he saw it nestling safely, he ran on to the next plane, another Caproni, and did the same, hardly aware that German bullets were zipping by dangerously close to his head. After placing his third bomb, he raced back to Jimbo, who was sitting upright over the collapsed canvas bag, opening and closing both hands to show that they were empty.

Glancing behind him, Callaghan saw that there were no more troopers in the vicinity of the aircraft – they had all joined Peterson to pour fire into the hut – so he knew that they had all disposed of their bombs.

'How many bombs were in the bag?' he asked Jimbo.

'Twenty-three,' came the reply.

'Damn!' Callaghan growled in frustration. 'There must be at least thirty planes here. What a bloody waste!'

'Twenty-three planes knocked out isn't bad,' Jimbo said. 'Assuming, of course, that the bombs go off. I think we'd better pull out now.'

Callaghan checked his watch. 'Five minutes to zero,' he said. 'Yes, Jimbo, let's go.'

Though pleased that twenty-three bombs had been planted, Callaghan still could not bear the thought of not doing more damage. Thus, as he was beating a retreat with the other men, still aiming a fusillade of fire at the barracks to keep the Germans pinned down as long as possible, he could not control himself when he saw the glow of instrument lights in the cockpit of a Caproni that obviously had just been worked on.

'Damn it!' Callaghan exclaimed, staring hungrily at the glowing aircraft. 'If I can't bomb another of those bastards, I'll take it out with my bare hands.'

'No, boss!' Jimbo bawled over the sound of his own roaring tommy-gun as the Germans poured out of the distant barracks. 'Those planes are about to blow up!'

Ignoring him, Callaghan raced across the airstrip

to the glowing Caproni, even as the German troops were also heading in that direction.

Some of the Germans stopped to take aim and fire at Callaghan, but as they did so, the first Lewes bomb exploded, blowing the wing off a Junkers, setting fire to its fuselage, then igniting its oil and making it erupt with a mighty roar, spewing jagged yellow flames and billowing black smoke.

Callaghan was climbing onto the wing of the Caproni, to get at the cockpit, when another Lewes bomb exploded, setting fire to a second Junkers, followed almost instantly by a third explosion, which blew a hole in the side of a Caproni. The heat of the fires beat back the advancing Germans, then obscured them in oily smoke, enabling Callaghan to reach the cockpit of the Caproni, where, in a fit of mute fury, he ripped the instrument panel out with his bare hands. Other Lewes bombs were exploding in quick succession, destroying more planes and filling the night with fire and smoke, as Callaghan threw the instrument panel to the ground, then followed it down. He glanced around him with pleasure as more aircraft exploded, then followed Jimbo and the others, now using the pall of smoke to give them cover as they raced away from the airfield.

Knowing that there was no time to lose, after reaching the head of the column Callaghan set a punishing pace for the march back to the desert RV. Rising to the challenge, and with little more to carry than their personal weapons and ammunition, the men kept up the pace and had soon left the airfield far behind. When they glanced back over their shoulders they could only make it out by the crimson glowing in the sky caused by the fires, and by the spasmodic, fan-shaped, silvery light of further explosions.

Reaching the general area of the RV, where they had expected to find the lorries, the men were briefly but dangerously confused by lights which at first they thought were being waved by the LRDG. In fact, they were torches being flashed by the Germans and Italians who had come in pursuit of them, losing them in the darkness and now circling blindly around them, unaware of their presence.

Callaghan used a hand signal to order his men the lie belly-down on the desert floor, where they stayed, making no sound, until the lights from the Axis vehicles had moved off to the west. When they had disappeared completely, heading away from the SAS men, Callaghan let the latter stand up again and use the whistling signals they had devised for attracting the LRDG in the desert's darkness.

Eventually, while Callaghan was carefully following his compass course, he heard the first whistled replies. Heading in that direction, he eventually saw the dark outline of the LRDG lorries, none of which had its headlights on. Drawing closer, he saw some of the men waving.

'A sight for sore eyes,' he said.

'Too right,' Jimbo agreed.

'I'm dying for a bloody drink,' Frankie informed them, 'so let's waste no more time, lads.'

As the SAS troopers hurried across the starlit plain, the LRDG soldiers stepped out to greet them like long-lost brothers; a lot of backs were slapped, hands shaken and congratulations offered.

'Twenty-three hits? Bloody terrific. Here, have a drink, mate!'

Desperately thirsty, Frankie was one of the first to be handed a water bottle by one of the Rhodesian drivers. He swallowed a huge mouthful before realizing, as his throat burned and he almost choked, that the water bottle contained rum. Recovering, and ignoring the laughing Rhodesians, he drank even more, then passed the bottle to his good friend Jimbo.

'When you get right down to it,' he said, 'there's nothing like water – pure, clean water.'

After drinking deeply from the same bottle, Jimbo felt obliged to agree.

'Great water!' he said.

Both of them slept like the dead throughout the long, rough journey back across the desert to the Jalo Oasis, where they were awakened by welcoming bursts of gunfire and cheers from most of their mates.

Even as Callaghan was marching to Stirling's tent to submit his report, Lewes and the men of S2 Patrol were on the road to El Agheila.

13

Because El Agheila was only half the distance from Jalo Oasis that Stirling had had to travel, Captain 'Jock' Lewes did not set out with S2 Patrol until two days after him. He was, in fact, just beginning his journey as Stirling and Callaghan were being brought back from Sirte and Tamit by the LRDG.

Lewes led his convoy of trucks out of Jalo with a great deal of pleasure, delighted to be back in action at last. Ever since serving in Layforce's No 8 Commando in Syria, he had gained a taste for adventure and was more easily bored than he had ever been. A low boredom threshold had always been one of his problems, but now his tolerance for inactivity was non-existent. Though superficially quiet and thoughtful, Lewes was a man of restless energy and vivid imagination who had to be kept engaged all the time.

While the early training of L Detachment in

Kabrit had kept him busy and satisfied – perfecting parachute landings, studying the art of desert survival, even inventing the bomb named after him – there could be no denying that since arriving at the Jalo base, where Stirling had been forced to wait for the right time to launch the raids, Lewes had almost gone mad with boredom. He had, of course, filled the time with more desert training and weapons practice, but those could not compensate for the real thing and his patience had worn thin.

Now, as he was driven out of Jalo Oasis by his LRDG driver, Thomas 'Tom Boy' Cook, he felt almost joyous.

This was regardless of the fact that the burly NCO in the rear seat, LRDG Sergeant Brendan McGee, did not approve of Lewes's insistence that they travel in this wonderful old Lancia staff car instead of an LRDG Chevrolet lorry.

'The Lancia's a fancy car all right,' McGee had sternly informed him, 'but it's not one to get you through the desert. Take a Chevrolet, sir.'

'I don't want a lorry, Sergeant. I want a bit of fun in my life and this car's just the ticket.'

'You're the boss, but don't ask me to approve. Be it on your own head.'

'Oh, stop being so po-faced, Sergeant McGee.

The Lancia will be perfectly fine, and that's what I'm travelling in.'

Lewes was wrong. The Lancia was, at least initially, a disaster. Everything was fine and dandy as they raced across the perfectly smooth, hard sand of the vast desert plain, but as soon as they reached an area of soft sand and gravel, the Lancia began bogging down and had to be dug out.

Though clearly infuriated, as his purple face showed, Sergeant McGee said nothing, other than to snap orders at his men as they slaved and sweated at this murderous task. Lewes, highly embarrassed, avoided his sergeant's steely gaze and concentrated on his map-reading. But when, a couple of hours later, they had to pass through an area of rippling sand dunes and the car bogged down three times over a distance of ten miles, Sergeant McGee's steely gaze had turned white-hot and was burning through the back of Lewes's neck.

'Don't say, "I told you so",' Lewes finally said to break the chilling silence.

'No, sir,' McGee replied. 'I won't say I told you so.'

'I was wrong, Sergeant. My fault. I apologize. I should have bowed to superior experience and not let my schoolboy's love of sporty-looking cars blind me to reason.'

McGee sighed, smiled a little, and stroked the bonnet of the Lancia as it was pushed by some troopers off the last of the sand mats and steel channels, back onto hard ground. 'I must admit, it's a beauty,' he confessed. 'It's just in the wrong place.'

Relieved, Lewes ordered the resting men back into their vehicles, then the convoy took off again, heading across a mercifully flat, hard plain, into the deepening crimson light of dusk. By last light they were well on the road to El Agheila — at least halfway, according to Lewes's calculations — so they made camp for the night, first erecting triangular poncho shelters between the vehicles and the ground, then lighting fires to cook up hot food.

'What about Axis aircraft?' Lewes asked McGee, who was now more friendly towards him. 'Won't they see our fires?'

'They'll see them all right,' McGee replied, automatically looking up at the vast, magnificent, star-filled sky, 'but being out here, they'll assume we're a bunch of Arab nomads. No need for concern there.'

Apart from the usual whining mosquitoes, fat flies and innumerable creepy-crawlies, the night passed uneventfully. By first light the men were all up to have a quick breakfast, clear away all signs of the camp, and hit the road while the heat was still bearable.

The first couple of hours were painless, with the forward momentum of the vehicles creating a cooling wind. Also the men's mouths and nostrils were protected from the billowing sand by the fluttering *shemaghs* wrapped around their faces, leaving only their eyes exposed. By eleven, however, the sun was high in the sky and not even the beating, snapping wind could counter the fierce, draining heat.

Just after noon, when the column had managed to advance half the remaining distance to El Agheila without a vehicle bogging down – not even the Lancia – a great dark wall formed on the horizon directly in front of them. McGee, still sitting in the rear of the Lancia, leaned forward to tap Tom Boy on the shoulder and tell him to stop. As the driver was braking carefully to avoid becoming bogged down, McGee stood up in the back and signalled with his right hand for the rest of the column to stop too.

'What is it?' Lewes asked.

'See that big dark wall on the horizon?' McGee asked by way of reply.

'Yes.'

'Now listen. What do you hear?'

Listening, Lewes heard what sounded like a train emerging from a tunnel and approaching rapidly.

'Sandstorm!' McGee bawled. 'Everybody take cover!'

The more experienced LRDG men were out of their vehicles so fast that they took the SAS men by surprise. Certainly McGee was out of the Lancia, huddled on the ground beside it and unrolling his poncho even as Lewes was still putting his feet down. Glancing back over his shoulder, Lewes saw that great wall of darkness growing larger as it advanced, blotting out the whole horizon, making the desert floor shake dramatically, and now sounding even more like an approaching train. The sun was gradually obscured by great spirals of sand and eventually disappeared altogether, leaving darkness almost as deep as night.

The oxygen seemed to go out of the air and the flies were swarming and buzzing like crazy things. Lewes could hardly breathe. 'Get down here!' McGee shouted, waving him down as sand suddenly swirled howling around the captain.

When Lewes dropped down beside McGee, the burly sergeant threw his poncho over both of them and told him to hold his corner down tightly. Lewes did so just as the sandstorm, travelling at nearly 50mph, swept over the Lancia with a mighty roar, tearing and punching at the poncho, making the car rock dangerously, sucking all the air out of the enclosed space beneath the poncho, and blowing the sand in through every opening, no matter how slight.

Lewes's throat went dry and he had great difficulty in breathing. The roaring wind was deafening and filled his ears with stabbing pains. For a moment he felt that he was going to be picked up bodily and carried off by the storm. In the event, he escaped this fate.

The sandstorm took only minutes to pass on, but it seemed more like hours. Eventually, however, the noise and the wind abated, the sand settled down and the suffocating heat was replaced with breathable air. When McGee tugged the poncho away to let Lewes look out again, he saw the sandstorm racing towards the southern horizon, now very far away, growing smaller as it rapidly receded. The sun was reappearing in the sky as the swirling sand settled down.

'Christ!' Lewes said softly.

'Your first one?'

'Yes.'

McGee grinned. 'The first one always comes as a shock. *Now* look at your Lancia!'

Completely buried, the car resembled a small sand dune. This time, however, most of the Chevrolets had suffered exactly the same fate.

'Oh, God!' Lewes groaned in exasperation. 'We're going to have to dig this lot out.'

' 'Fraid so.'

After dusting themselves down, the troopers and LRDG men set above scraping the sand off the trucks with their bare hands. They had to do this before they could even get at the spades and shovels, buried with the rest of their kit. Once they had regained those, they were able to remove the sand more quickly, though it still took some time and, in the ferocious heat of noon, made them all sweat like pigs. Two of them were rendered nauseous by the heat and threw up in the sand. The digging took nearly two hours and was punctuated by a series of five-minute breaks to avoid further such problems. Even then, when the vehicles were cleared, they had to be pushed out with the aid of sand mats and steel channels. By the time they were ready to set off again, most of the men were exhausted.

'Do you think they'll be fit enough for the raid tonight?' McGee asked Lewes, obviously referring only to his SAS troopers, not to the more experienced LRDG.

'Yes,' Lewes replied without hesitation. 'They'll get their strength back just sitting in the lorries for the rest of the journey. We're nearly there, Sergeant, so with luck we should get there without any more problems.'

Luck was with them at last. The rest of the journey passed without incident and by last light they were on the outskirts of El Agheila, with the Gulf of Sirte visible in the distance, beyond the sandy cliffs of the coastline. Their luck then took a turn for the worse once more when, approaching the unguarded airfield under cover of darkness, they found no planes on the runway.

'Damn!' Lewes exclaimed softly, lying belly-down on the summit of a low ridge and studying the airfield through his binoculars. 'There's not a damned thing down there. Just a few huts and a couple of Kraut and Eyetie soldiers. That isn't an airfield – it's just a bloody staging post for planes passing through.'

'I fear so,' McGee replied, also studying the empty runway through binoculars. 'It's been rumoured that the Axis air forces have begun dispersing their planes to fields where they can be properly guarded. I think that's happened here – and if that's the case, the planes won't be coming back. As you say, this is probably now just a staging post for aircraft that have to land temporarily, probably for refuelling. Apart from that, it's inoperative. You can tell that by the lack of facilities and the small number of guards. It's been a wild-goose chase, Captain.'

Lewes rolled onto his back; placed the binoculars on his belly, and gazed up at the stars. 'Buggered if I'll have this,' he said, suddenly sitting upright and hanging the binoculars around his neck. 'I'm not going to waste *my* bag of bombs. I want to see them put to good use.'

McGee sat up beside him. 'What does that mean, Captain?'

'According to our intelligence reports, there's a building not far from here, in Mersa Brega, where the German top brass regularly conduct intelligence meetings. I'm going to find that building, Sergeant, and blow it to hell.'

'That's taking a mighty big chance, Captain.'

'That's what life's all about. Are you with me?'

McGee shrugged. 'Why not?'

The men, many of whom were as disappointed as Lewes, were ordered back into the vehicles and followed the Lancia away from the airfield, heading back for what was marked on the map as an Axis MSR. When they reached the road, which was certainly wide enough for heavy-duty military traffic and raised a few feet above the desert floor, they parked a good way from it, hidden in the darkness at the bottom of the sloping ground. While waiting, the men ate their wads and drank hot tea from vacuum flasks. When a sizeable German convoy rolled past on the road above, they hurriedly packed away their remaining wads and the vacuum flasks, started up the engines and followed the Lancia up onto the road.

With a daring that took even Sergeant McGee's breath away, Lewes urged Tom Boy to drive faster until he had caught up with the tail of the German column, where he insisted that he remain for as long as possible. In fact, they stuck to the tail of the column, with their own column of LRDG lorries strung out behind them, until the convoy reached Mersa Brega.

If any of the men in the German column looked back, they must have assumed, in the darkness, that the Lancia and the lorries behind it were their own.

'I've got to hand it to you, Captain,' Sergeant McGee said, his eyes never moving from the back of the German lorry directly ahead. 'Apart from your unfortunate choice of cars, you're a cool-headed officer.'

'I try to be,' Lewes replied.

Eventually the German convoy reached a fenced

compound, beyond which was a single large brick building and a vehicle park. The first vehicles in the column slowed down, stopped, then started moving into the compound one by one, passing heavily armed guards.

'This must be the place we want,' Lewes said. 'It wouldn't be so well guarded otherwise.'

'Are we going in?' McGee asked in disbelief.

'We can try. We won't be noticed until we reach the guardhouse. The second we get there, we open fire with our small arms, picking off the sentries, then race into the compound with the rest behind us. We can shoot up the building as we approach it and then bomb it to hell.'

'Christ!' McGee said, though he grinned with pleasurable anticipation and unslung his tommy-gun from his shoulder. 'Did you get all that, Tom Boy?' he asked the driver.

'Yes, sir!' Corporal Cook replied. 'The minute we get to the guardhouse, I put my foot down.'

'Make sure you do, Tom Boy.'

In fact, the Italian sentry at the guardhouse recognized the British markings on the Lancia just before it reached the open gates. He bellowed a warning and lowered his rifle as the siren on the guardhouse started to wail. Tom Boy instantly put his foot down and roared towards the gate, hard on the tail of the German lorry that had just passed through.

Meanwhile Lewes unholstered his Browning High Power handgun and put two bullets into the sentry. The impact threw the Italian backwards into the wall. As the Lancia swept past the guardhouse, Lewes emptied the handgun into it, in the hope of cutting down the other sentry.

Glancing back over his shoulder, he saw the other LRDG lorries racing between the open gates, one after the other, with some of the men also firing at the guardhouse with their semi-automatic weapons, causing showers of wood splinters to fly off it and almost certainly killing anyone still inside.

Tom Boy braked sharply, going into a skid, when he saw that the German lorries up ahead had stopped and were disgorging their heavily armed soldiers. As the Lancia skidded to a halt, the LRDG lorries coming up behind spread out around it and also slid to a standstill, allowing the SAS troopers to pour out, already firing their small arms at the advancing Axis soldiers.

'Damn!' Lewes rasped, hauling the bag of bombs onto his lap and looking ahead at the Axis soldiers fanning out across the compound and blocking the way to the brick building. 'We'll never get past them.' He glanced sideways at the parking area, which was filled with dusty troop lorries and gleaming staff cars. Bullets zipped past his head in both directions, being fired simultaneously by his SAS troopers and that formidable mixture of Germans and Italians. 'So!' he said. 'If we can't blow up the building, we'll destroy as many vehicles as possible. Come on, Sergeant, let's go.'

He jumped out of the Lancia, still holding the bag of bombs. McGee did the same, then hurried around the back of the car to join Lewes, who was rummaging about in the bag, taking out as many of the small bombs as he could carry. He then handed the heavy bag to McGee. 'Distribute these to some of the other men and tell the remainder to keep those soldiers away from us.' He had to shout above the general bedlam, to which was suddenly added the sharp roar of Tom Boy's Sten gun, which the driver was firing from the front seat of the Lancia.

Glancing at the Axis troops, Lewes saw some of them dropping, but the others were still returning the SAS fire while gradually spreading out across the compound.

'We're going to have to be quick,' McGee said.

'Then get going, Sergeant!'

While the SAS troopers kept the Axis soldiers busy, Lewes ran towards the parking area. By the time he reached it, McGee had distributed the Lewes bombs and the troops armed with them were running forward to join Lewes. They spread out, planting bombs on lorries and staff cars alike, and managed to complete the job before the enemy troops could head in their direction.

As each man planted the last of his bombs, he ran back to rejoin his own lorry and add his firing to the increasingly ferocious barrage aimed at the enemy.

One SAS trooper fell, then another, and a third. The Axis troops were falling at a greater rate, but that was not encouraging. Leaving their dead where they were lying, the SAS men backed towards their own lorries, firing as they retreated, and scrambled up into them. The last men were still hauling themselves up, or being hauled up, as the lorries turned around on screeching tyres and raced out of the compound.

The time fuses on the Lewes bombs had been set for the minimum delay of ten minutes. As the last of the LRDG trucks roared out of the compound, Lewes glanced sideways from the Lancia, out on lead, and saw the Axis troops hurrying towards the parking area to remove the bombs.

Lewes crossed his fingers.

The first lorry to explode did so with a thunderous noise just as the enemy troops were approaching. It went up in smoke and flames, blowing apart, spewing metal, forcing the Axis troops to throw themselves to the ground or beat a hasty retreat. The lorry was followed by a staff car, then another lorry, then another, until the area had become a spectacular inferno of vivid-yellow flames, black, boiling smoke, melting rubber and flying, spinning, red-hot metal.

The Axis troops could do nothing but watch the continuing destruction – so shocked that they made no attempt to pursue the men who had caused it.

As he raced away in his Lancia, Lewes looked back with pride, counting ten, twenty, then thirty Axis vehicles either destroyed completely or seriously damaged.

'That makes up for a lot,' McGee said.

Lewes heard cheering from the SAS troopers in the trucks behind him. He uncrossed his fingers and stuck his thumb up in the air as the lorries headed back to Jalo Oasis, over 120 miles away, beyond the moonlit horizon.

14

Lieutenant Greaves was scheduled to raid Agedabia airfield just before the Oasis Force's advance, due to start on Tuesday 20 December. Brigadier Reid and his staff had worked out that by Wednesday the Force would be nearing the area of regular Axis air patrols. Therefore anything Greaves could do to hamper these, particularly by destroying enemy aircraft, would be of invaluable help to the campaign.

'We can't make that advance if the number of Axis planes aren't greatly reduced,' he said. 'That's the job of L Detachment, Lieutenant, and failure isn't acceptable.'

Greaves left Jalo Oasis with only two of his own men, Corporal 'Taff' Clayton and Private Neil Moffatt, a few hours before Stirling returned. The group, driven by an LRDG private, Bob Purbridge, had a reasonably uneventful journey to Agedabia, with only a couple of punctures to contend with; and each mile that took them closer to their target was also, Greaves suddenly realized, taking him back to where he had been before meeting Stirling: in that great Allied camp located just outside Mersa Brega in the vast desert of Cyrenaica.

That had only been seven months ago, but it seemed more like seven years. Three days after Greaves had been casevacked from Tobruk, Rommel's Panzer divisions had cut off the port. Seventeen days after that, while Greaves was recovering from surgery in the Scottish Military Hospital in Alexandria, German troops had occupied Halfaya Pass and the British had been forced to retire across the border into Egypt. A month later, when the British attempted to take the Pass back with Operation Brevity, they were defeated again.

By the middle of June, when Greaves was still recuperating in hospital in Alexandria, the British attempted to relieve Tobruk with Operation Battleaxe, but were quickly forced back to the starting line. In July, a few days after Captain Stirling was moved into the bed beside Greaves, General Claude Auchinleck replaced General Wavell as Commander-in-Chief in the Middle East. Then in November, when Captain Stirling, admirably energetic even when on crutches, was telling Greaves about his idea for small raiding parties, another major British offensive intended to defeat the Axis forces in Cyrenaica and free Tobruk, began with a series of confused battles around Sidi Rezech, but ended with more gains for the Germans.

Now, in late November, the major battle for control of the Western Desert had begun and Stirling's dream of small raiding parties had become, at least in principle, a reality. Whether or not the raids would be successful was another matter entirely.

They'd better be successful, Greaves thought grimly as his Chevrolet raced across the vast, featureless plain, taking him closer to Agedabia, only 40 miles from Mersa Brega, where the retreat had begun. If they don't, he thought, the fate of L Detachment will be sealed and Stirling's dream will be smashed. The SAS will be no more.

Shocked by that idea, Greaves straightened in his seat and glanced at the setting sun, going down like pouring lava and spreading its crimson fire across the horizon, bringing darkness to Tunis and Tripoli and the Gulf of Sirte, to the unforgettable blue of the Mediterranean and the desert's dazzling whiteness. The other raiding parties, he knew, had already done what they could do in that same protective darkness – at Tamit, at Sirte, and at Agheila – but whether or not it had been worth it he had yet to find out.

Had they succeeded or failed? Had they lived or died? Would he ever see Stirling, Callaghan, Lewes or any of the others again? Indeed, would he himself return from this mission? That, too, he would soon find out.

'There's the sea, Lieutenant,' Private Purbridge said. 'That must be Agedabia.'

'It is,' Greaves replied.

He glanced all around him at the vast, darkening desert, seeing, due east, nothing but mile upon mile of featureless mile but for the black lines of distant dunes; and, due north and north-west as far as Tripoli, the glitter of sea sinking into sunset. It was difficult to accept that this vast, barren wasteland joining Tripolitania to Cyrenaica was filled with the tanks, lorries, armoured cars and seasoned troops of the legendary General Rommel's Panzer divisions. In the silence of the desert's failing light there was no sign of war.

Nevertheless, Greaves reflected, they are all around us, so we must be careful from now on.

'The airfield's just over that ridge, due north-west,' he told Purbridge. Drop us off near the top of the ridge, where we should still be out of sight.'

'Will do, Lieutenant.'

Five minutes later the lorry was bouncing over a mixture of soft sand and gravel as it made its way up the gentle slope of the low-lying ridge. Just before it reached the top – where it would have been silhouetted against the skyline – Private Purbridge braked to a halt.

'Home and dry,' he said.

Greaves and the other two clambered out, carrying their small arms. Taff then picked up the bag of Lewes bombs and slung it over his shoulder. Greaves walked the few steps to the edge of the ridge, peered down through the darkness, then returned to the lorry.

'It's too dark to see much from here, so we'll have to start hiking willy-nilly.' He checked his watch, then spoke to Purbridge. 'Without knowing just how far away the airfield is, or how well it's guarded, I've no way of knowing how long this is going to take or when we'll get back. My suggestion, therefore, is that you wait here until first light. If we're not back by then, assume we've been captured or shot and drive yourself back to Jalo. If, on the other hand, you hear sounds of activity – gunfire, sirens or, hopefully, our exploding Lewes bombs – you can assume we're in the thick of things and will be attempting to make our way back. In that case, keep your eyes peeled for us and prepare to get going. Understood?'

'Yes, sir.'

Greaves turned to Taff Clayton and Neil Moffatt. 'Right, lads, let's get going.'

With that, he led them over the low ridge and down the dark, gentle slope at the other side, marching towards the airfield. It was not an easy march. In fact, the area surrounding the airfield was patrolled constantly by German troops, both on foot and in lorries, so the SAS men had repeatedly to drop to the ground, faces pressed to the soft sand, and wait for the patrols or trucks to pass, silently praying that they would not be seen. Naturally, this made their advance on the airfield slow and nerve-racking. Eventually, however, they reached the perimeter and found it not only securely fenced, but patrolled by the crack troops of the Panzer Grenadier Regiments of the 90th Light Division.

'This is not going to be easy,' Greaves whispered as he knelt behind a sandy ridge, beside Taff and Neil, a good half mile from the wire. 'We have to get across that flat stretch without being seen, then somehow get through the wire. Not easy at all.'

'What I'd like to know,' Taff said, 'is ...' He coughed into his fist. 'Is it actually possible?'

Surprisingly, it was the solemn, almost anonymous Neil who gave them the impetus. 'Of course it's possible. We just advance an inch at a time, belly-down on the ground, stopping every time we spot a guard or when those searchlights come in our direction. It might take us a little bit of time, but in the end we'll get there.'

'You think so?' Taff asked doubtfully while scanning that distant wire.

'Yes,' Neil replied firmly, yet glancing at Lieutenant Greaves for support.

'I agree,' Greaves told him. 'Besides, what else can we do? We can't turn back now.'

'Just watch me,' Taff said. 'I'll be out of here like a bat out of hell.'

'I'm not dragging this bag of bombs anywhere,' Neil solemnly informed him, 'except through that wire.'

'Well, Corporal?' Greaves asked, giving Taff the choice.

Taff sighed. 'Oh, what the hell? Yes, sir, let's do it.'

'Good man,' Greaves said. He glanced at the heavy bag of bombs. 'You won't be able to drag that with you, so let's divide them up between us right now. How many are there?'

'Thirty-five,' Taff said.

'*What?*'

'Thirty-five.'

Greaves sighed. 'Right, Corporal, that's eleven to you, eleven to Neil and thirteen to me. But how the hell do we carry them?'

'There are smaller bags inside this one,' Taff said. 'We take one bag apiece.'

'Excellent. Quick, man!'

Taff opened the big bag, pulled out three smaller bags, divided the small Lewes bombs into three piles, with two extra for Greaves, then put them into the separate bags and gave the heaviest to Greaves. Each man then slung his own bag onto his back and tied it to his shoulders with its fixed cords. They were now all set to leave.

'Right,' Greaves said. 'Let's go.'

They moved out immediately, first running at the crouch but soon forced to drop to the ground and crawl forward, first on hands and knees, then belly-down. This was both tedious and arduous, every yard a struggle. Thirty minutes after starting they were already feeling the strain and realized that they had advanced only a little. Slithering like snakes down a sand-and-gravel slope to the bed of a dried-up wadi, they took a short break, tried to ease their aching muscles, then began the crawl up the other side. Reaching the top and peering over the rim, they saw that the area between there and the perimeter was literally swarming with German troops.

'Jesus!' Taff whispered.

'I don't care how long it takes,' Greaves said, also whispering, 'but we're going to go through that damned wire. Any arguments, gentlemen?'

Taff and Neil did not argue.

It took four hours, for they advanced an inch at a time. The guards marched to and fro, and the searchlights swept the terrain, as the three SAS men snaked forward on their bellies, stopped, started again and repeated this pattern endlessly, feeling like worms in the earth, but obliged to continue, working their way unseen to the wire.

First one hour, then two, and still with half the journey to go. At one point a truck raced past them so close it spewed sand over them; at another they had to lie as still as corpses for an hour with Germans and Italians congregating yards away. The Axis troops lit cigarettes, conversed in their separate languages, shared a flask of water or wine, then finally wandered off in opposite directions, letting the SAS men advance again – a very slow advance, the so-called 'leopard crawl', painstaking and stealthy.

The third hour ran interminably into the fourth

and they had finally made it. They were right at the fence.

Greaves checked his watch and saw that it was nearly midnight, which just made him feel more tired.

Checking left and right, he saw that the nearest guarded entanglements were quite a long way off and that the searchlights were hitting the ground well away from the fence. Relieved, he rose to his knees and removed a small pair of wire-cutters from his webbed belt.

'Have you got the same?' he asked Taff and Neil.

'Yes,' they replied simultaneously.

'Good. Get to it, lads.'

Between them they managed to cut through the wire in no time, taking care that it did not shake too much, lest it attract the attention of the guards at the entanglements on both sides. When the wires had been parted, they left the cutters on the ground – they were now an unnecessary burden – and made their way quietly through the opening, heading straight for the airfield.

Probably because the wired perimeter was so heavily guarded, there were no guards on the air-field itself, nor on the parked aircraft, which were mostly CR42s, an Italian biplane fighter-bomber.

'A gift from God!' Greaves whispered, smiling delightedly at Taff and Neil. 'When you've planted all your bombs – or if Jerry sees any of us before we've done so – head straight back to the opening and try to make your way back to the lorry. Good luck, lads. *Go!*'

They all scattered in different directions, heading out in triangular formation to work their way down the three rows of planes. They went from one plane to the next over the next forty-five minutes, placing their thirty-five bombs one by one, each man waving to the others each time he planted one, before moving on to the next plane. No one came near them. Nor did they see any Axis sentries. The job took all that time, but it was easy to do, and when they had disposed of all their bombs, they met under the wing of one of the last two planes, the three of them as happy as Larry.

'We're short of two bombs,' Neil said.

'Damn!' Greaves exclaimed.

'If these thirty-five bombs go off,' Taff said, still grinning, 'I won't complain about the two short.'

'Those fuses are set for sixty minutes,' Neil reminded them, 'so we'd better get going.'

'Shit, yes!' Taff said.

In fact, the bombs began exploding before they cleared the airfield, five minutes earlier than anticipated. Most went off at the same time, some only slightly later, and the combined effect was spectacular, creating a stunning display of searing white flames and billowing smoke, accompanied by a cacophony of explosions composed of the actual bombs and the igniting petrol tanks of the planes. Within seconds the whole airfield resembled a modern version of hell, with flames eating into flames, smoke spiralling and billowing upwards to form immense, oily black clouds, and burning rubber, melting perspex and red-hot metal spewing skywards and raining back down.

Luckily, by then the three SAS men had already made it to the barbed wire, gone through the opening, and were running at the crouch back into the darkness unseen by the Germans, most of whom were racing the other way, towards the unexpected hell of the airfield.

This time, since they did not have to crawl on their bellies, Greaves and his two companions covered the same distance in an easy thirty minutes instead of an arduous four hours. When they got back to the ridge, Purbridge was waiting for them, the engine of the Chevrolet already turning over.

When they were safely in their seats, he took off – in the words of Taff – like a bat out of hell.

15

With all the raiding parties back in Jalo Oasis, Captain Stirling called a meeting between his officers to discuss their various adventures and decide what changes to their techniques had to be made in the light of their experience. Gathered around the long trestle table in Stirling's large tent, the officers smoked like chimneys, drank a lot of whisky or beer, swapped jokes and informal conversation, then eventually got down to serious business.

'So what was this problem you had coming back, Dirk?' Captain Stirling asked Lieutenant Greaves.

'Once we'd completed the raid,' Greaves told him, 'we laid up most of that night, then started across the desert the next day. Everything went smoothly – not a German in sight – until, still deep in enemy territory, we were mistaken for an Axis patrol by two of our own Blenheims.'

'Damn!' Stirling exploded.

'They attacked us with their guns,' Greaves continued, recalling it vividly, with anger, 'and though I and my two men managed to get out of the lorry in time, one of the Blenheims stitched it with bullets and killed the LRDG driver, Private Purbridge, before we could exchange recognition signals.

'Bloody rotten luck!' Lewes exclaimed softly.

'Those RAF prats!' Callaghan added with some venom.

Greaves just shrugged his shoulders. 'When the pilots finally recognized us and flew back where they had come from, we buried Purbridge in the desert. Private Moffatt of L Detachment then took over the driving.'

'You navigated yourself?' Lewes asked him.

'Yes.'

Callaghan gave a low whistle of admiration, then glanced at Lewes. 'Your training wasn't in vain, then,' he said.

'So what happened next?' Stirling asked impatiently.

'Unfortunately,' Greaves continued, 'one of the Blenheims had shot up the petrol tank and though we managed to patch it up temporarily, it was losing fuel at an increasing rate and the engine was gradually packing up. As luck would have it, later that day we reached Wadi Faregh, where Brigadier Reid's Force was passing through to their night laager some 25 miles from the airfield. They fixed us up with another lorry and driver, so finally we made it back here.'

'An absolutely tragic end to a successful raid,' Stirling said. 'My condolences, Dirk.' He was, however, keen to hear some good news. 'So how, precisely, did the raid go?'

'Perfect,' Greaves said with some pride. 'The place was heavily guarded and we had difficulty getting in – at least it took a long time – but we didn't have a single encounter with the enemy while planting our bombs.'

'The bombs all went off?' Lewes asked anxiously.

Greaves smiled at him. 'Perfectly, Jock. A little earlier than planned, but that may have turned out to be a blessing. Certainly Jerry had no time either to remove them or come looking for us. We practically *walked* away from that airfield as the planes were all blowing up.'

'*All* of them?' Stirling asked.

'We were two bombs short,' Greaves said, 'which made me a little angry. But, as Corporal Clayton pointed out, thirty-five hits out of thirty-seven is no cause for complaint.'

Stirling nodded. 'Quite right.'

Lewes wasn't so happy. 'I'll have to check the fuses,' he said of his own invention, the Lewes bombs. 'Yours weren't the only ones to go off early.'

'Right,' Callaghan said. 'Ours were set for thirty minutes, but they went off in twenty, nearly accounting for us with the aircraft.'

'We didn't even get the chance to try ours,' Stirling confessed bitterly.

'Oh, why?'

'Damned aircraft at Sirte took off before we could launch the raid. All thirty of them. Leaving us with all those unused bombs. So,' he said, changing the subject, 'what *was* the success rate?'

'We got twenty-three planes out of thirty,' Callaghan said, 'and only failed to get the rest because we ran short of bombs.'

'We didn't get any aircraft at all,' Lewes confessed, 'but we destroyed or seriously damaged thirty Axis vehicles.'

'We got thirty-five out of thirty-seven,' Greaves said, 'and like Captain Callaghan's group, we only failed to hit the others because we ran short of bombs.'

'Bloody stupid!' Stirling said angrily. 'Another

example of lack of proper planning and intelligence.' He drummed his fingers on the table, looking distracted, then had a slug of whisky and perked up. 'Nevertheless, looking on the bright side, in a single week we destroyed a total of fifty-eight enemy aircraft, thirty enemy vehicles, and one enemy oil-tanker. We also caused a lot of disturbance and kept their troops distracted. Not bad at all, gentlemen!'

Stirling topped up his glass, passed the bottle around the table, then held his glass out in a toast. 'To the first successes of L Detachment, SAS,' he said. When the officers had toasted their own success, they drank more whisky, lit up more cigarettes, filled the tent with smoke, and returned to the more serious business of the rights and wrongs of the raids.

'Any complaints about the LRDG?' Stirling asked.

'None,' Callaghan said.

'They were perfect,' Lewes added.

'No one could have done it better,' Greaves insisted. 'They were bloody marvellous.'

'I concur,' Stirling said. 'The failures are all down to us, so we have to address that fact.'

He glanced outside the tent where the other ranks were either bathing in the pools of the oasis or relaxing under the palm trees, drinking and smoking as well, but also reading or writing letters home. The sun was blazing out of a sheer blue sky, making the vast, flat desert look almost white.

'In future,' he said, turning back to the officers smoking and drinking around the table, 'we have to try to avoid the kind of disaster that befell us at Sirte. In order to do this, we have to ensure that we have good intelligence beforehand.'

'Hear, hear,' Callaghan said.

'Here are just a few of the things that went wrong,' Stirling continued, counting them off on the fingers of his right hand. 'Some of our targets flew away before we could get at them. We had no idea if the airfields we targeted were guarded or not. Captain Lewes turned up at an airfield that was, in fact, merely a staging post containing no aircraft. We should have known these facts in advance.'

'Right,' Lewes said.

'Another damaging delay was caused by the simple fact that two Arab girls decided to tend their garden. This also could have been avoided with prior intelligence. In short, we should have known about that garden.' Stirling glanced at each of the men in turn, letting them know he was serious. 'And there were, alas, other silly mistakes.'

The officers glanced uneasily at one another

when Stirling deliberately paused for dramatic effect.

'Captain Callaghan, for instance, made the mistake of firing at the enemy before his men had planted their bombs, thus alerting the garrison to what his group was doing.'

'Sorry about that,' Callaghan said. 'I just got carried away.'

'Please don't let it happen again, Paddy.'

'I won't, boss, I promise.'

'Captain Lewes ignored the advice of his experienced LRDG sergeant and took a vehicle unsuited to the terrain.'

'Guilty,' Lewes said. 'I stand corrected.'

'He also engaged the enemy before planting his bombs, thus running the risk of alerting them to what was happening. In his case, the circumstances were mitigating, but again, if we'd had proper intelligence, he wouldn't have turned up at an empty airstrip and had to go elsewhere.'

This time Lewes made no comment.

'Regarding the timing of the raids, in future we'll also have to make allowance for the unexpected, such as the sandstorm that delayed Captain Lewes's patrol.'

'A terrible experience,' Lewes said, 'albeit a brief one.'

227

'As for myself,' Stirling continued, 'I must confess that I was careless enough to trip over an Italian sentry who then alerted the whole damned garrison. Had that not happened, we might have attacked the airfield earlier and the planes would not have flown away before we could get to them. I believe this happened because I was too tired – but I shouldn't have been. I should have laid up the night before the raid to ensure that I was fully alert. I, too, stand corrected.'

His fellow officers smiled at that.

'So,' Stirling summarized, 'in future, whenever possible, a number of guidelines will be followed. No raids will be mounted until the targets have been fully recced and accurate intelligence is received. No recces will be made without a day's lying-up before the raid. The raiders will not engage in gun battles *before* they've planted their bombs. The fuses of the bombs will be double-checked for precise timings. The number of targets must be accurately ascertained and no patrol will have a shortage of bombs. All future schedules will incorporate allowances for unexpected desert phenomena, such as sandstorms and the bogging down of vehicles. Last but not least, with regard to being shot at by our own bloody aircraft, the pros and cons of disguised vehicles will have to be looked into before we make any further raids. I think those are the lessons we've learnt, gentlemen. Are there any questions?'

'Yes,' Callaghan said, bored already and eager to get back to work. 'When and where are the next raids?'

'As it's clear that the success of the raids depends on surprise, we'll strike next where the enemy will least expect us.'

'Where's that?' Lieutenant Greaves asked.

'Exactly where we raided before,' Stirling, in better mood, replied with a wicked schoolboy's grin. 'At Sirte and Tamit — but approaching by a different, more westerly route.'

'When?' Captain Callaghan asked impatiently.

'A couple of weeks from now,' Stirling told him. 'To be precise, Christmas Eve.'

'My Christmas present!' Lewes said.

16

By the time Stirling's raiders moved out again the situation in the Western Desert of Cyrenaica had again changed dramatically. The 5th South African Brigade had been annihilated by the Afrika Korps south-east of Sidi Rezegh; fierce fighting then took place between the Axis forces and the New Zealand Division; General Ritchie's Eighth Army sustained heavy casualties, but still managed to weaken the Afrika Korps, causing Rommel to withdraw his forces from the Crusader battle rather than let them be destroyed; and finally, on 10 December, Tobruk as relieved and the Afrika Korps began its retreat, first to Gazala, then as far south as El Agheila. Stirling's raiders, therefore, in leaving the Jalo Oasis on Christmas Eve, even as units of the Eighth Army were advancing on Benghazi, found themselves travelling towards the southern flank of the retreating Axis forces, under skies filled with

Axis and Allied aircraft, all flying to and from the battle zone.

'To get to our targets,' Stirling said to Captain Halliman, 'we're going to find ourselves practically in the lap of the Axis forces now dug in around Agheila. This could be rather tricky.'

'Damned right,' Sergeant Lorrimer said from the rear seat, where he was sitting as Stirling's second-in-command.

Even as they were speaking, the faint throb of engines made them squint up at the sky where they saw a fleet of Handley-Page Halifax four-engine bombers heading north to pound Rommel's forces.

'Good lads,' Stirling murmured.

As before, he was travelling with S1 patrol, commanded by LRDG Captain Gus Halliman. This time, however, instead of targeting only Sirte, the plan was for Stirling's raiding party to be dropped off within hiking distance of Sirte while another, led by Captain Callaghan, would make a return journey to Tamit for a second attack based on the wisdom of hindsight. When the two raids were completed, both teams would meet up with the LRDG lorries at a desert RV due south of the targets.

Meanwhile, a third raiding party led by Captain Lewes, with Lieutenant Greaves as second-in-command, was being transported by the LRDG

T2 Patrol, mostly composed of New Zealanders, to Nofilia, over 120 miles east of Sirte, where they would launch a simultaneous raid.

The first day's journey across the vast, flat plain passed uneventfully and with even less punctures than before, because the LRDG, after their previous experiences, were now using specially reinforced tyres. As usual, the men were all wearing *shemaghs* to protect their faces, not only from the fierce heat, but also from the billowing clouds of sand churned up by the lorries' wheels. These, however, did little to alleviate the sweat that soaked through their clothing. Nevertheless, as they gazed across the vast expanse of the desert, seeing the cliffs of the upland plateaux beyond the heat haze in the north and the golden sand dunes framed by azure sky in the west, few of them were immune to the desert's lunar beauty and most realized they would never forget it.

This time they passed a few Arabs on their camels, desert traders carrying their wares to other Arab camps irrespective of the aircraft overhead or the tanks and armoured cars massed to the south. Seen in the distance, with their loose robes fluttering, wobbling precariously on their camels, distorted by the heat haze shimmering up from the desert floor, the Arabs looked archaic, ever unreal.

'You wouldn't bleedin' credit it, would you?' Jimbo said to his mate, Frankie, sitting beside him in the rear of one of the Chevrolets as it carried them across the burning sands. 'Those bleeders haven't changed in a million years and aren't likely to. Here we are with our tanks and armoured cars and aircraft, fighting with 25-pounder guns and semi-automatic rifles, and those bastards are still crossing the desert on camels with nothing but swords on their hips. Fucking unbelievable!'

'Right,' Frankie replied, yearning desperately for a fag but not able to light one because of the wind beating at his face. 'One minute you're looking at the blackened wreck of a Daimler armoured car or Sherman tank, all rag and bone inside; the next you see an A-rab on a flea-ridden camel and you think you're hallucinating from the heat.'

'Or a mirage,' Jimbo said.

'I see *them* all the time, mate. Great pools of water, naked women, pints of bitter, plates of roast beef and Yorkshire pudding. I see 'em and smell 'em night and day. That's what this place does to you.'

'Know just what you mean,' Jimbo said.

That night, when the trucks were laagered, the men erected their standard triangular poncho tents between the vehicles and the ground, put up (and rushed to use) the thunderboxes, then lit a few camp-fires and used petrol-can cookers to make their own fry-ups of bacon rashers, tinned tomatoes and bread, the eggs being too fragile to carry.

Alas, when these more pleasurable activities had been exhausted, they were compelled to undertake the more tedious, yet vitally necessary, chores. For the men of L Detachment, SAS, it meant removing their bolt-action rifles, semi-automatic weapons and machine-guns from their wrappings of stretched condoms, cleaning them yet again, no matter how minute the traces of sand found in them, and then wrapping them up again for another day's travel across the desert.

'That's the first time I've ever used a contraceptive,' Neil confessed. Then, realizing what he had said, he blushed a deep crimson.

'Ho, ho!' Frankie roared.

'The secret's out!' Taff added.

'Virgin, are you?' Jimbo asked him with a sly grin. 'So no use for a rubber?'

'Course not!' Neil insisted, blushing an even deeper crimson. 'I just don't use a johnny, that's all. It deadens the sensation, my girl says.'

'Mmmm,' Jimbo responded, grinning slyly at Frankie. 'Deadens the sensation, does it? What do you do, then? Pull out before you come?'

'Hey, come on, Jimbo!' Neil protested, pretending to be involved with his kit, this giving him an excuse to keep his head down and hide his reddening cheeks. 'You don't ask a bloke that kind of thing!'

'Yes, you do. I've asked Frankie here. We're mates and that's what mates talk about. Isn't that right, Frankie?'

'It is,' Frankie replied, pleased to be discussing Neil's virginity instead of his own. 'Mates shouldn't have secrets from one another, after all. What are friends for, if not for sharing their little secrets?'

'Right,' Taff said emphatically. 'So come on, Neil, let us have the filthy facts. If you don't use a johnny, how do keep your little bit of fluff from getting a bun in the oven?'

'Show some respect, Taff!'

'We're your friends. We'd like to know.'

'Why don't you try guessing?' Neil said as if disdainful, though actually trying to hide the fact that he did not have a clue, for he had never got that far and assumed the other three had.

'We'd like you to tell us,' Frankie insisted, artfully hiding the fact that he, too, was a virgin and had only ever used a condom to protect his rifle.

'I respect my girl too much,' Neil lied shamelessly.

'Do you *know* what to do without a johnny? Have you ever unwrapped one, kid?'

'Aw, come on, Jimbo! Knock it off! Of *course* I've unwrapped one. I just don't like to use them, as I said, and that's all I'm saying.'

'So what do you do?' Jimbo insisted. 'Pull it out before you come? Do you squirt it all over her lovely belly and make a right bleedin' mess?'

'God, you're disgusting! I'm not listening to this.' Neil stood up and glanced across the desert like a man deep in thought. 'I think I'll go for a piss.'

Neil snorted, then stomped away from the camp to take a leak out in the desert, well away from the mocking laughter of his mates. 'Filthy-minded bastards!' he muttered as he stepped into darkness, suddenly filling up with visions of his girlfriend back home in Blackburn. A pleasingly plump lass who worked in the cotton mills, she had frequently let him feel her breasts in the back row of the local cinema, but had never let him go any farther, always whispering, 'Not until we're married, luv!' Neil was not sure that he loved her, but he certainly wanted to marry her, if only to feel more of her, and now all that talk about johnnies was making him think of her.

Suddenly he felt very far from home and yearned to be back there, even if only for a short while, back in the back row of the cinema, feeling Florence's soft breast.

'Those bastards!' he muttered as he spread his legs and irrigated the sand of the vast, moonlit darkness just outside the perimeter of the camp. 'They've got no sensitivity.' Nevertheless, he felt an awful lot better when he had emptied his bladder.

Meanwhile, the navigators were using the abundance of stars to check their position and plot the next day's course. Their calculations would, however, be double-checked at first light the next day with the aid of a compass and sextant.

Bored out of their minds with no one to torment, Jimbo and Frankie, having been taught a few things by their LRDG navigator, the amiable Rhodesian, Mike Sadler, watched him at work with his sextant. Inspired by his performance, they decided to experiment with improvised compasses by stropping razor blades against the palms of their hands, as Mike had taught them, and dangling them on lengths of thread to see if they pointed north.

'Mine's stopped,' Jimbo said. 'It's pointing north.'

'How do *you* know?' Frankie asked. 'Could be south, for all you know.'

'Wherever it stops is north, you bleedin' berk!'

'So how do you know?'

''Cause Mike told us so.'

'Mike's a bloody Rhodesian,' Frankie said, 'and they're all mad as hatters and born liars. He was pulling your leg.'

'It's fucking north,' Jimbo said. He studied the dangling razor blade for a moment, not really seeing it, his thoughts focused on sex, this having been brought on by all that talk about contraceptives.

Now, with a hard-on, brought on by sexual taunts, Jimbo suddenly realized that he had not had it for a long time – certainly not since leaving Cairo a couple of months ago. Instead, he had been forced to toss off a lot and make his own right bleedin' mess in the desert sands. Bloody shameful, when you thought of it, what a man had to do, no matter how hard he tried avoiding it. Human nature was base, all right.

Still tormented by his hard-on, which was only made more insistent by recollections of the many delicious little whores he had had in Tiger Lil's in the Sharia el Berka (all the time trying desperately not to think of his wife in Wapping), Jimbo tried to distract himself by recollecting how, during one weekend in Cairo, he had tried to distract himself from the temptations of Tiger Lil's by visiting the Great Pyramid of Cheops, located on the west bank of the Nile.

'Pretty bloody mysterious, isn't it?' he said, tapping the dangling razor blade with his forefinger and watching it slowly spin before pointing north. 'I mean, the way a magnetized razor blade will always point north.'

'I wouldn't know if it's mysterious or not,' Frankie responded pragmatically. 'I just know it does.'

'Bloody funny things, razor blades,' Jimbo said, trying to lose himself in higher thoughts. 'Remember that day I visited the Great Pyramid?'

'No.'

'Well, I did, see? And you know what I found out?'

'No.'

'Well, I visited the Great Pyramid because I'm interested in certain mysteries, see? Like Ancient Egypt and the stars and what have you. And when I visited the Great Pyramid I learnt, from this old Arab who guided me, that if you put a razor blade inside the pyramid between shaves, it'll never go blunt. In fact, if you keep puttin' the razor blade in there between shaves, you could use the same razor blade for ever. Bloody amazing, isn't it?'

'Fascinating,' Frankie replied. 'I'm amazed that half the population of Egypt isn't lining up every night to leave their razor blades in the pyramids

and save themselves a fortune in the long term.'
He tapped his dangling razor blade and watched
it spinning. 'Fucking rubbish!' he said.

Later that evening they stretched out on their
groundsheets, but found it next to impossible to
sleep, being tormented by buzzing flies and whining
mosquitoes, as well as haunted by the thought of
creepy-crawlies, particularly snakes and scorpions.

'I keep thinking I can feel things crawling over
me,' Frankie complained. 'I'm not scared of the
Krauts, I don't mind dying by the bullet, but I
have to confess my nerve collapses completely
when I think there's something crawling up my
leg, heading straight for my balls.'

'Stop being so bleedin' childish,' Jimbo remon-
strated. 'You're supposed to be superior to common soldiers, so try to act like you're . . . *Christ,
what's that?*'

'What?'

'Fucking hell!' Jimbo frantically rolled off his
groundsheet and turned back to examine it. 'Something nipped me,' he said. 'A bleedin' scorpion! I'll
be dead by first light . . . Whoops!' He reached
down and snatched at it. 'Here's the little bugger! A
stone as sharp as a fucking razor. All right, Frankie,
stop laughing.'

Later, when it grew colder and even the flies and mosquitoes had settled down, they were kept awake by the bass rumbling of heavy bombers overhead and, for an hour or so, by a *son et lumière* spectacle of tracer shells and bomb explosions illuminating the north-western horizon over what they could only assume was El Agheila, where the Afrika Korps had dug in.

'War can be so beautiful,' Captain Halliman said to Stirling where they lay side by side under a triangular poncho tent strung between their lorry and the ground.

'You think so?'

'Yes. It has a kind of terrible beauty, but the beauty of it can't be denied. I suppose that's what makes war so seductive – it startles and stuns. Rather strange, don't you think?'

'No,' Stirling replied. 'I don't think it's strange at all. Everything seductive is dangerous – and that's what war is.'

'Seductive?'

'Yes. It's rather like mountaineering, which I've done quite a bit. The higher you go, the more dangerous it becomes. The more dangerous it becomes, the more beautiful the world looks and the more heightened your senses become. I would call that seductive.'

241

'You've climbed some dangerous mountains, haven't you?'

'Yes,' Stirling replied.

'Those climbs must have heightened your senses in a truly dramatic way.'

'They did. They made me feel supremely alive. The desert can do that as well – as can the war we're conducting here.' He glanced at the horizon, where explosions and burning fires were streaking the sky with criss-crossing lines of red, yellow and purple, now visible between pyramids of pulsating, silvery, eerie light. 'That spectacle on the horizon is part of all that. It means death, but it's beautiful.'

Halliman sighed. 'It certainly reminds me that they're dying while we live . . . and *that* certainly makes life seem all the sweeter.'

'You only truly appreciate life when you've come close to losing it,' Stirling said. 'Few are privileged to do so.'

They both slept on that notion.

Up at first light the following day, the men had a quick breakfast of wads and hot tea, then dismantled their shelters, rolled up and packed their groundsheets and ponchos, poured petrol on their own waste and burned it, and in general removed all traces of the camp.

Moving out with the vehicles spaced well apart, in single file, just like a foot patrol, the column soon reached the southernmost tip of the Western Desert, where many battles had raged back and forth over the past few months. It was therefore no accident that the men soon found themselves passing through an eerie flat, white landscape littered with the blackened wreckage of bombed tanks, armoured cars, troop lorries and half-tracks, both Axis and Allied, with whole areas of flatland given over to mass graves covered with hundreds of crude white crosses.

'We're south of El Agheila,' Captain Halliman explained. 'We're now heading north to Sirte and Tamit. We'll be there quite soon, David.'

Surprisingly, though the sky overhead was filled with aircraft, both Axis and Allied, the column was not attacked and eventually, just before last light, they reached the DZ for the first raiding party, to be led by Stirling.

After clambering down to join the rest of his group, Stirling walked over to Callaghan's lorry to wish him good luck.

'Don't forget,' he added, 'that even as we speak, General Ritchie's Eighth Army is advancing on Benghazi and might, indeed, wrest it back from the Afrika Korps today. Because of this, our recent intelligence will be relatively useless. What I mean is that the situation will be changing every minute and we've no way of knowing whether or not the planes we've targeted are going to be called into action, thus leaving us again with empty runways. Also, more importantly, we've no way of keeping in touch with the Axis troop movements, which means we could run smack-dab into them. For this reason, then, no matter what happens, just try to do as much damage as you can, as best you can, wherever you can, then get the hell back to the desert RV. That's it, Paddy, good luck.'

'The same to you, David.'

The LRDG lorries moved off across the desert, churning up clouds of sand that obscured the sinking sun. Stirling waited until they had disappeared completely, then turned to his men.

'Right, chaps, let's get going. Irregular single file behind me. Jimbo, you're out on point as lead scout. You, Frankie, are coming up the rear as our always dependable Tail-end Charlie. Does that sit well with you?'

'Yes, boss,' Private Turner replied, pleased to be called by his first name and to use the word 'boss' in return, instead of the usual 'sir'. Frankie had never liked the rigidity of normal Army protocol, which is why he had applied for L Detachment.

This new, informal approach, particularly when combined with the unusual nature of the work, made him feel pretty good. 'Tail-end Charlie it is,' he said, then turned away and went to the back of the column to take up his position.

Captain Stirling raised and lowered his hand, indicating 'Move out'.

Beginning the hike at sunset, they arrived in protective darkness at the road that ran west of Sirte, beyond which lay the airfield. Once there, Stirling's luck, if such it could be called, changed for the worse yet again.

Just as they approached the road, advancing in single file, intending to cross it one by one, the lights of a slow-moving vehicle appeared in the north, where the coastline lay, and came inexorably towards them.

Stirling signalled immediately for the men behind him to lie down, then he too fell to the sand, just behind Jimbo Ashman. The latter, being an experienced soldier, was already flat on his belly by the edge of the road, holding his Sten gun at the ready.

The lights came towards them, advancing along the road. As they came closer, other lights floated into view behind them, then more lights behind those. They floated eerily in the darkness, beaming down on the road. Gradually gaining in definition, they turned out to be the lights of troop lorries. The first rumbled past, then the next, a third and fourth. Behind the fourth lorry was a German armoured car, followed by a tank.

Stirling sighed in despair. His raiding party was trapped at the side of the road by an Afrika Korps armoured column moving up to the front. It was composed of hundreds of vehicles, including tanks, armoured cars, half-tracks and troop lorries, and it was carrying thousands of men.

It took four hours to pass.

Lying there belly-down by the side of the road, Stirling was convinced that he was going mad. The armoured column passed at a snail's pace, hundreds of vehicles, one by one, and he checked his watch compulsively, obsessed by the time, realizing that *his* time was running out and that soon he would have none left to spare. The strain was almost intolerable, but he had to bear it, wondering meanwhile what the men behind him were thinking as they, too, lay flat on the ground and watched their opportunities slip away.

When, four hours later, the last of the German vehicles had passed, Stirling realized that there was not enough time left to go on to the airfield. He had been foiled again.

'Damn, damn, damn!' he whispered, hammering his fist into the sand.

'You said it yourself, boss,' Sergeant Lorrimer consoled him. 'The Crusader battle has made everything unpredictable and we've no way of knowing what to expect. Let's do what we can, while we can, wherever we can, then get the hell out of here.'

Charmed to have his own words flung back at him, Stirling smiled again.

'Damned right,' he said.

'So?' Lorrimer asked, always keen to present a challenge.

Stirling checked the time again. 'Because that bloody armoured took four hours to pass, we have approximately sixty minutes left to cause some mayhem and madness. Let's do it, Sergeant.'

'I'm here to obey orders, boss. Just give me the word.'

'Weaponry?'

'This time, just in case, we brought along a Browning 0.5-incher and a Bren light machine-gun. The men, apart from those, are reasonably well equipped, with a combination of bolt-action rifles, tommy-guns, and that new thing, the 9mm Sten sub-machine-gun. Not too many worries in that direction, boss. No need to sweat.'

'Land-mines?'

'Absolutely.'

'Hand-grenades.'

'Naturally.'

'You've just made my day, Sergeant Lorrimer. Let's get set to hit and run.'

'It's as good as done, boss.'

'We need transport.'

'I'll call it up.'

Having brought along a No 11 radio set, Lorrimer used it to recall one of the LRDG lorries that had gone on to Tamit. Twenty minutes later, even before the arrival of the vehicle, a German staff car came along the road with a full complement of top brass. Placed in charge of the Browning 0.5-inch machine-gun, Jimbo had no hesitation in squeezing the trigger and sending a hail of bullets into the German officers. They died amid a convulsion of flailing limbs as their vehicle, also peppered with bullets, careered off the road, dived nose-first into the sand and exploded when its petrol tank was punctured.

'We've just given our position away,' Stirling said, sounding pleased, 'so let's hope that LRDG lorry gets here and takes us elsewhere.'

Luckily, it did. Five minutes after the destruction of the German staff car, which had burst into flames and was pouring oily black smoke, an LRDG lorry arrived to hurry them out of the area.

'Take us ten miles down the road,' Stirling said, 'towards the enemy lines. That way, we can pick the bastards off before they get this far. Nipping them in the bud, as it were. A bit like gardening, really.'

Once driven along the road by the LRDG corporal, they planted some land-mines across the desert road, actually an MSR, then spread out again belly-down on the ground and waited for more Axis traffic to pass. The next time it was a troop lorry packed with Italian soldiers. It was blown up by the land-mine, flipped onto its side, and started burning as the unfortunate troops spilled out onto the road. There, before they could even scramble onto their feet, they were chopped to pieces in the triangular fusillade of bullets from Jimbo's 0.5-inch Browning and the Bren light machine-gun being fired by Frankie.

The Italians ran left and right, dropped to their knees, crawled on their bellies, some trying to unsling their weapons, many shouting curses or orders, but the triangular hail of bullets made the ground spit and explode, first around them, then between them, filling the air with swirling sand, and they screamed, convulsed and jerked like demented puppets, then fell back into the murk, their clothing in tatters, punched with holes, torn to shreds, and often died beneath the bodies of their comrades, who were falling like nine-pins.

'You're not bad at all,' Jimbo said to Frankie, both men oblivious to the screams of the wounded scattered around the blazing Italian troop lorry. 'You're pretty good really.'

'Those two bastards are born killers,' Lorrimer told Stirling. 'I'm not suggesting it's good, I'm not complaining that it's bad, but I'm certainly saying they're the kind we're looking for. Take that as you may, boss.'

'I take it as read,' Stirling replied. 'Now let's move on, Sergeant.'

They moved on along the road, heading towards the enemy lines, and again took up their positions on both sides of the road. This time they hit an Italian tank, first stopping it with land-mines, which blew its treads off, then punching holes in its side armour and fuel tank with a combined burst from the Browning 0.5-incher and a Bren light machine-gun, and finally slaughtering the crew in a hail of fire from their combined bolt-action rifles, tommy-guns, and 9mm Sten sub-machine-guns as the unfortunate men, some on fire and already screaming dementedly, tried to escape the series of convulsions that were filling the interior with flames and smoke.

When the attack was over, with nothing left alive in the pall of smoke covering the burning tank and road, the SAS men moved on again.

So it went for the next few hours, a precise routine repeated constantly, with the men attacking Axis transports along the MSR, using a combination of land-mines, machine-guns, and automatic and semi-automatic rifles which, between them, created a devastating cross-fire. Tanks exploded internally. Lorries burst into flames. Staff cars careered off the road and rolled over in clouds of dust, the officers inside peppered with bullets that ricocheted off the doors, shattered the windows, and in general created a bedlam that drowned out the screams of the dying. Other soldiers, not so lucky, were incinerated in the flames, choked in the dense smoke, or expired slowly in the agony of amputated limbs and punctured stomachs. Very few survived.

Leaving the smouldering wreckage and its dead, Stirling's group advanced even closer to the Axis lines to attack again, exactly as previously – land-mines for the vehicles, machine-guns and small arms for the troops – before those travelling in the direction of Sirte could find the previous victims.

As the vehicles included tanks, armoured cars, half-tracks, staff cars and lorries, the results of Stirling's attacks along the MSR, moving ever closer to the front, were more impressive than even he realized at first. Certainly, by the end of the few hours left to him after being stopped by the four-hour-long convoy, he had caused an enormous amount of damage to the Axis transports attempting to move along the MSR.

'I couldn't have picked them off easier at a funfair in Brighton,' Jimbo said to Frankie as they packed up their machine-guns and moved out. 'A regular little duck-shoot, that was. We should do it again sometime.'

They moved out with minutes to spare, heading back across the desert, leaving their last victims sprawled across the wide MSR in a welter of burning petrol, melting rubber, buckling perspex, smouldering upholstery, shattered glass, and red-hot, twisted metal. They also left the stench of cordite and scorched flesh, heading gratefully back into the pure air of the clean, silent desert. The buzzing of flies and the whining of mosquitoes did not count in this reckoning. Now the desert seemed pure to them.

Four hours later, in the early hours of the morning, Stirling arrived back at the desert RV, where Callaghan, already sitting in his poncho tent with a glass of whisky and cigar, told him that his group had destroyed a whole squadron of aircraft on the airfield at Tamit.

'A real fireworks display,' he told Stirling. 'Flame and smoke to the heavens.'

'That sounds like Irish hyperbole,' Stirling replied, 'but being Scottish, I'm pleased to accept it. Pour me a whisky, thanks.'

'L Detachment, SAS, has earned its wings,' Callaghan told him. 'You need doubt it no longer.'

Stirling looked up at the vast, starlit sky and asked his one, burning question: 'Where are the others?'

17

Dropped off by T2 Patrol at Nofilia, over 120 miles east of Sirte, Lewes made for the airfield under cover of darkness with Lieutenant Greaves and his troopers, including Corporal Taff Clayton and Private Neil Moffatt, determined to prove the worth of his bombs. Unfortunately, as before, the problem was not the bombs, but the shortage of targets and the lack of adequate prior intelligence.

With the best will in the world, Lewes could do little at Nofilia because there were only a few Axis planes on the runway, so widely dispersed that it took an age to get from one to the other. To make matters worse, the need to tie the SAS raids to General Ritchie's advance on Benghazi had left no time to correct the erratic timing of the Lewes bomb fuses. Thus, the bomb on the first plane, timed to ignite in thirty minutes, went off much earlier, before the raiders were even clear of the second plane.

That first bomb exploded as the men were making their getaway, thus drawing the Axis sentries to the airfield. Even worse: the second bomb never went off – either because the fuse had malfunctioned or, just as likely, because the early explosion of the first bomb had given the enemy warning in good time to either defuse, or remove completely, the second bomb.

In any event, by the time the single explosion erupted behind them, illuminating the night sky with jagged fingers of yellow flame that were almost instantly smothered in a blanket of ink-black smoke, Lewes and Greaves were already racing away from the airfield, to begin their trek back across the desert to the RV. Glancing back over their shoulders, they saw the flames and smoke of the burning plane, with Axis troops converging from all sides to the scene of the blaze.

'Only one!' Lewes exclaimed bitterly. 'Not even two!'

'It's the luck of the draw,' Greaves responded. 'Come on, Jock, keep running!'

They fled from the unguarded perimeter as fast as their legs would carry them, glancing repeatedly back over their shoulders to check that the Axis troops now surrounding the blazing plane had not decided to follow the saboteurs. In the event, none of them did, which made the getaway easy. Nevertheless, the SAS men slowed down to a quick march only when the airfield behind them was out of sight beyond a line of smooth, wave-like sand dunes painted pale white by the moonlight. When the dunes too had disappeared, the men slowed down to a normal walk.

'What a bleedin' cock-up!' Taff said to Neil, just before they broke into single file. 'I thought we'd really bought it that time, mate, what with all those bleedin' Germans flooding over the runway when that bomb went off early.'

'I was saying my prayers, I can tell you,' Neil replied solemnly. 'Nearly shitting my pants, I was. We were lucky they all went for that burning plane and didn't come after us.'

'One fucking bomb! It breaks your bleedin' heart.' Taff could hardly believe they'd had such bad luck. 'So much for so little!'

'Not as bad,' Neil said. 'One bomb's better than none – and it kept the Germans and Eyeties busy, at least.'

'Look for the silver lining, right? You're a bloody optimist, Neil.'

'I like to look on the bright side, that's true. So what happens now?'

'We're going to the RV. Linking up with Captain Stirling and other raiding parties that were sent off on raids in the same area at approximately the same time. Then the LRDG lorries will take us back to base and a nice cup of char.'

'I can't wait,' Neil said.

In fact their jocular manner hid a bitter disappointment that nagged remorselessly at all of them as they made their long march through the night.

The desert's darkness was deep, though a pale moon shone down, and the silence had an unreal, eerie quality that made some of the men uneasy. Planes often flew overhead, obviously heading for Benghazi, and occasionally lorries were heard in the distance, taking troops to the front. Lights fanned up in the distance, illuminating the northern horizon, reminding the men that the war was still engaged and that the planes overhead were on bombing runs against the beleaguered Axis forces.

'It looks pretty from here, doesn't it?' Taff said. 'But I bet it's hell over there.'

'We're marching in the right direction,' Neil told him. 'Well away from that shit.'

'Poor bastards,' Taff said.

'Move apart, you men!' Lewes snapped. 'You're supposed to be marching in single file, not bunched up like Girl Guides.'

'Sorry, boss!' Taff responded, then fell back to where he was supposed to be – as Tail-end Charlie. He felt isolated back there, cut off by the moonlit darkness, too aware of the vastness of the desert and its lack of identifiable features. He felt minute and vulnerable.

Lewes, meanwhile, though second in the group, now marching behind Neil, was emotionally isolated by his nagging sense of failure, unable to believe that they had managed to bomb only one Axis plane. Even worse: either one of his bombs had failed to go off or the early ignition of the first one had given Jerry time to defuse the second. Either way, Lewes had little to be proud of and was feeling extremely bitter about it. He marched, then, in disconsolate isolation, blaming himself, but also gearing himself up for further research into explosives and other tactical matters when he got back to the base camp at Kabrit.

L Detachment, SAS, is now a functioning, worthy unit, he thought, but it's not perfect yet. Making it perfect is the next job on my list. I must keep this in mind.

That his interest was returning already had to be a good sign.

They marched for six hours, but still arrived at the desert RV in darkness, just before first light. As usual, they made contact with the LRDG by using a series of whistling sounds, which both groups recognized, then by shining their torches at those shining at them. Eventually, the lorries of the LRDG took shape in the darkness and the other men, including those of the SAS, came forward to greet them.

Stirling, towering over most of the others, was the first to emerge from the darkness, holding his hand out and smiling. He shook Lewes's hand and asked, 'How did it go?'

'Badly,' Lewes replied bluntly.

He told Stirling what had happened. Stirling listened thoughtfully, then smiled even more widely and patted Lewes on the back. 'Nothing to be ashamed of, old boy,' he said. 'These little mishaps are bound to happen and have to be lived with. Look at us, after all. We didn't even get as far as the airfield.'

'But you made up for it,' Lewes said, 'by attacking Jerry along that MSR.'

'We were in the right place at the right time.

That's all there was to it. Come on, Jock, cheer up! It's Christmas morning, after all. Also, we've just heard on the radio that General Ritchie's Eighth Army marched into Benghazi yesterday. Our raids, so I'm told, had a lot to do with that – reducing the number of enemy aircraft and distracting their troops – so we've finally proved our worth to the sceptics. L Detachment, SAS, is now a viable entity. They won't stop us now.'

'Well, that's something,' Lewes said.

Feeling a lot happier when he climbed up into the heavily armoured, four-wheel-drive Chevrolet, behind Sergeant McGee and his driver, Corporal Cook, he was glad to take his usual seat right beside the Boyes anti-tank gun mounted in the rear and manned by Private Sammy Bakewell of the LRDG.

The rest of the men were still greeting each other, shaking hands and slapping backs, trading compliments or amiable insults, when Stirling took his place in the lorry of the LRDG commander, Captain Halliman.

'Looks like we're leaving straight away,' Jimbo said, where he stood with Frankie, Taff and Neil near the lorry that was taking them back.

'Without even breakfast,' Taff complained.

'You didn't earn breakfast,' Jimbo told him. 'I mean, one plane for Christ's sake!'

'You didn't get *any*,' Neil reminded him.

'So? At least we shot up a lot of bleedin' Krauts and Eyeties, as well as their tanks, armoured cars and troop lorries. That's more than *you* did.'

'You bastards just struck it lucky,' Taff insisted. 'It's as simple as that.'

'Right!' Jimbo said. 'Begrudge us our dues. Just because you can't face the fact that your own raid was a bloody balls-up. It's understandable, really.'

'One plane,' Taff insisted, 'is one more plane than *you* bastards got.'

'Don't come it, m' darling!'

'Get up on your trucks, you bloody men!' Sergeant McGee bellowed. 'We haven't got all day!'

Startled, Jimbo and the others hurriedly climbed up into their lorries to a round of sardonic applause from the other men.

'Thank you, folks,' Jimbo said, taking a bow. 'And now for our next act!'

Up in the leading vehicle, the LRDG commander, Captain Halliman, with Captain Stirling by his side, raised his right hand and waved it forward, indicating that the convoy should move out. The engines roared into life, the wheels churned up clouds of sand, and the lorries headed across the flat plain, towards the first gold-and-crimson tendrils of the rising sun.

Within half an hour the sun was a huge red-and-yellow ball in a whitening sky. An hour later, it was just a fierce whiteness in a sky of the same colour. The cold of night was burned away, the heat was rising rapidly, and the air was filling up with the usual buzzing flies and whining mosquitoes. These came swarming around the troopers every time the trucks stopped for their hourly checks. They got under the men's *shemaghs*, into their cups of tea, and covered their uniforms and weapons. A normal day in the desert.

'Open your mouth to drink your char and you're going to have *these* bastards for breakfast,' Jimbo said, swatting flies and mosquitoes from his cup. 'I can take anything the desert throws at me except these bloody insects.'

'You've just managed to speak without swallowing them,' Frankie replied, 'so they can't be that bad.'

Frankie never bothered swatting them away; he seemed to think they were natural.

'You're a walking dung-heap,' Jimbo told him. 'That's why they don't bother you.'

Frankie grinned and patted Jimbo on the shoulder. 'My old mate,' he said.

They had stopped for one of their hourly vehicle

checks when Sergeant McGee, hawk-eyed as ever, spotted a plane glinting in the sky and bawled a warning to everyone.

It was an Italian Savoya SM 79 Sparviero, a light bomber with three 12.7 Breda machine-guns and a Lewis gun, as well as over a ton of bombs. It flew directly over them, circled back, then banked and flew at them.

'He's attacking!' Captain Halliman bawled.

The Italian pilot flew in low, all his guns spitting fire, stitching lines of exploding sand across the desert, running at tremendous speed towards the parked trucks. The men in the trucks returned fire with their Boyes anti-tank guns and Lewis light machine-guns, but the Savoya was already releasing its first bombs and climbing as the bullets from its guns ricocheted noisily off the lorries and wounded some screaming men.

The bombs seemed to drop slowly, turning over like black slugs, then hit the ground and exploded, one slightly behind the other. The earth erupted into two roaring mushrooms of sand, soil and smoke.

When the smoke and raining sand had thinned out, the blackened, mangled remains of an LRDG lorry was revealed. It had been blown up, set on fire, and turned upside down, with its passengers either killed by the blast, burned alive or crushed to death.

'Bastards!' Jimbo bawled, standing up in the rear seat of his own vehicle, beside the Boyes gun, and shaking his fist at the Savoya as it circled around in the distance, coming back to attack again. 'Fuck you!' he screamed, unslinging his Sten gun and preparing to fire at the oncoming plane. 'Have a mouthful of this!'

The Boyes and Lewis guns roared again as the Savoya banked towards the column and began its second descent. The yellow flickering along its wing edges indicated that its guns were firing, then two more bombs dropped from its belly and fell like black slugs as the lines of spitting sand, kicked up by bullets, raced towards the column.

Jimbo was not alone in opening fire with his Sten gun. Most of the SAS men were on their feet, in the lorries or beside them, adding the roar of their rifles, semi-automatics and even handguns to that of the LRDG machine-guns.

The second pair of bombs exploded as the Savoya roared overhead, its bullets peppering more of the men and ricocheting off the lorries. The earth erupted again, one explosion following the other, to pick up two vehicles, smash them together, and throw the passengers in all directions, like rag dolls, before the lorries crashed back to the ground.

The mushrooming clouds of sand, soil and smoke briefly blotted out the sky, eventually rained back down, and drifted away on the wind, revealing more death and devastation, with charred bodies smouldering in the wreckage.

When the Savoya circled around and banked for another attack, Lewes, enraged, took charge of the pintle-mounted Lewis light machine-gun. After swinging it expertly onto what he deemed to be the proper elevation, he waited until the aircraft was virtually roaring straight at him with yellow fire spitting from its wings.

Lewes opened fire as twin lines of spitting sand raced up to his lorry, ricocheted off its bonnet, and blew the back of McGee's head off. Perhaps Lewes saw the spewing brains, blood and bone of the sergeant's exploded head before bullets punched through his own body like a series of red-hot rivets, throwing him violently backwards off the lorry and into the sand. After that, he saw nothing.

The two bombs from the Savoya, which roared overhead and away, exploded in front of the truck, picking it up and flipping it over, to smash back down in geysering sand that covered Lewes like a blanket.

Stirling jumped from his truck and ran back to examine Lewes. Discovering that he was dead, he shuddered helplessly with grief and shock, then managed to regain control of himself, clenching and unclenching his fists repeatedly, letting the tension flow out of him. Finally, breathing deeply and wiping some tears from his eyes, he stood up over the dead body of Captain Lewes and scanned the silvery-blue sky.

The Savoya had gone but he knew that it would return, almost certainly bringing other aircraft with it.

Possibly reading his mind, Sergeant Lorrimer said, 'I think we should move on.'

'Yes,' Stirling said. 'I agree. However, I fear we can't take the dead with us. It's too hot for that.'

Lorrimer snapped his fingers at a group of SAS troopers standing nearby. 'You men,' he said. 'Get some shovels and bury these dead men – and be quick about it.'

'Yes, boss!' two of the men said simultaneously. Then they all went off to one of the trucks to get a couple of shovels. The six men were able to dig two shallow graves in a relatively short time. While they were digging, another couple of troopers wrapped the dead bodies of Captain Lewes and Sergeant McGee in tightly bound canvas sheeting.

Eventually, when all was ready, the bodies were lowered into the shallow graves and covered up again. After the men had solemnly gathered around the graves, Captain Stirling, clearly trying to hide his overbrimming emotions, conducted a brief, moving ceremony, completing it with an unsteady voicing of The Lord's Prayer.

Raising their heads after the prayer, the men saw Captain Stirling wiping another tear from his eyes before composing his features.

'That's it,' he said, trying to sound gruff. 'All right, men, let's go.'

The men piled back onto their lorries and continued the long drive due east, towards Jalo Oasis.

Unfortunately, as anticipated by Stirling, two German Me 109F fighters appeared on the horizon to finish the work begun by the Savoya. Suddenly roaring in overhead, one after the other, they turned the desert floor into a sea of spitting sand, then tore the earth up in a series of roaring eruptions when two sticks of bombs were dropped in close succession. The bombs exploded even as the jagged lines of spitting sand raced through the column and peppered the lorries with bullets that ricocheted off into the wild blue yonder, miraculously without hitting any of the SAS or LRDG troopers, most of whom were trying to bring the departing aircraft down with their small arms. The combined noise of the exploding bombs, roaring machine-guns, and automatic and semi-automatic weapons was ear-shattering, with the men continuing to fire even after the Messerschmitts had flown off, letting the swirling, billowing sand settle down around the still-moving convoy.

The men in the trucks cheered when they saw the planes flying off. They stopped cheering when they turned around and headed back towards them.

'They're coming back!' someone bawled.

A running game of hide-and-seek then began between the lorries and the aircraft and continued for the next few hours.

At times the lorries would try to race away from the planes with the LRDG gunners firing on the move; then the lorries would be called in to form a defensive laager, when the fire of the LRDG gunners would be joined by a fusillade of fire from the small arms of the defiant SAS troopers.

The tyres of one vehicle exploded, making it sink to the ground to be obscured in billowing clouds of sand. Another was peppered with bullets, was hit in its petrol tank, and exploded into flames as the last of its crew jumped to safety. Another lorry was picked up and flipped over by a bomb explosion, tipping its crew out, then finally crashing upside down, practically bouncing off the desert floor, and finally grinding to a halt in a hole created by its own weight, like a dying animal digging its own grave.

Eventually most of the lorries were damaged one way or another by the enemy aircraft, but miraculously no more men were hit and the drivers kept going.

Running out of ammunition, the Messerchmitts flew off.

They were replaced, however, forty minutes later by the original Savoya, which again caused havoc with its deadly combination of spitting machine-guns and exploding bombs.

Knowing that a defensive laager would be a sitting duck for the Savoya's bombs, Captain Halliman ordered the other drivers to scatter as widely as possible across the desert, thus forcing the Italian pilot to choose between individual targets.

He was, in fact, coming in on a low sweep over Halliman's lorry when six RAF Hurricane II fighters, probably en route to El Agheila, spotted him and banked to attack him. Four of them bore down upon him, one after the other, all with guns roaring, and the Savoya shuddered violently, belched out oily black smoke, lost pieces of one wing, then went into a spinning, shuddering, whining dive to the desert floor, where it exploded in a spectacular ball of vivid-yellow fire surrounded by boiling black smoke.

As the scattering Chevrolets of the LRDG came back together again, the Hurricanes flew over them, dipped their wings in salute, then flew on towards the coast, eventually disappearing beyond the horizon.

'We all complain about the RAF,' Lieutenant Greaves said to Jimbo, 'but sometimes, you must admit, they're worth waiting for.'

'I hate to admit it,' Jimbo replied, 'but those bastards *did* warm my heart.'

Lorrimer, listening in on the conversation, just shook his head wearily.

The LRDG lorries continued on towards Jalo Oasis, though by now they were all virtual wrecks that began breaking down, one after the other. As each vehicle expired, its passengers would clamber out, strip the vehicle of anything of value – usually tyres, petrol cans and water –

and distribute themselves and the spare parts as evenly as possible between the others lorries. Then the ever-diminishing convoy would trundle on across the flat, sun-scorched plain.

Gradually, however, the remaining lorries also broke down, until, by the late afternoon, there were only three left, with fifteen men on each, balanced precariously and holding on to each other in a pile of salvaged tyres, petrol cans, water bottles, and weapons. Another vehicle then broke down, leaving only two, which meant that a lot of the men had to start walking, though mercifully now in cooling darkness.

By the time the cool air had turned to rapidly chilling night wind, another lorry had broken down and the sole remaining one, sagging under the weight of its fifteen men, was squeaking in protest as it crawled on.

Stirling and Greaves, though offered a lift on the last lorry, still in the charge of Captain Halliman, decided to set a good example to their men by rejecting the offer and joining the others on the arduous march through the freezing night.

After four hours, they caught up with the remaining lorry, which had expired trying to climb a slight slope, beyond which lay a broad swathe of perfectly flat, hard terrain, perfect for driving. The passengers were nowhere in sight, which meant they had marched on.

'If this was daylight,' Lorrimer said, 'you'd see their footsteps all the way across the desert, heading towards the horizon. They aren't waiting for anyone.'

'Good on 'em,' Taff replied. 'They've set a shining example.'

'Damned right,' Lorrimer said.

By first light, a total of forty-five men were spread out across the desert, all heading in their separate ways for Jalo Oasis. Though ragged, numb with cold, hungry and thirsty, none showed the slightest sign of wanting to give up.

'Not now,' Jimbo gasped. 'Not after all this shit. I'm only going down when I'm in my grave and that's a long way off yet ... Come on, Taff, stay awake!'

'It's my eyes,' Taff replied, croaking out of a ravaged throat. 'They're hurting so much from the sun, I can't keep them open. It's not tiredness – I don't think it's that – it's just my eyes that are giving in.'

'Your eyes? Shit! You're swaying like a reed in the wind and wandering left, right and centre. You're about to collapse, Taff.'

'I won't fall until you do.'

'We all heard you making that bold statement,' Frankie told him, 'so now you're going to have to live up to it.'

'Right,' Neil said. 'Here, put your arm around my neck . . . That's it, Taff! Now lean on me.'

'I'm all right, I tell you . . . Thanks, Neil. God, I'm so bloody tired!'

'We're *all* tired,' Jimbo said.

'Shut your mouths, conserve your breath and keep marching,' Lorrimer told them. 'That way you might make it back.'

So saying, he hurried on ahead, swinging his arms as if marching to a brass band, setting a shining example. It was his way of helping them.

Thus they helped one another, supporting each other, taking turns, and so managed to get through another night and into the second day. It was worse than the day before. The heat was like a furnace. The flies and mosquitoes, smelling sweat, sensing weakness, went into a veritable frenzy around the men, attacking in swarms. The light dazzled and blinded.

Sometimes a man collapsed. When this happened, others supported him. When that man recovered, smiling sheepishly, maybe shaking, he took his turn in supporting another man – and so it went on for many hours – even when the dazzling light and fierce heat of the day had returned to blister the skin around their eyes and drain them of strength.

It was only the *shemaghs* that prevented their faces from being blistered and gave them protection from the frenzied swarms of flies and mosquitoes. They marched, walked, stumbled and sometimes crawled through those noisy swarms, those veritable clouds of insects, emerging from them, as if from dark rain clouds, to the sun's dazzling light and the heat haze shimmering up from the desert floor. Scorched and consumed by the sun, they gradually merged with the featureless desert, becoming part of its landscape.

They were ghosts in the haze.

Captain Stirling stayed out in front. He felt that it was his duty. Already a tall man, he grew taller as the day began, letting his stature, both real and imagined, give strength to his men. They followed as best they could, some close behind him, others straggling, and were proud to see that the other officers – Captain Callaghan and Lieutenant Greaves – were marching as resolutely as himself, though now looking like scarecrows.

This is the final testing ground, Greaves thought, recalling the great battle outside Mersa Brega and thinking it child's stuff compared to this. If we finish this hike, if we survive, we'll have proved we are worthy. L Detachment, SAS, will exist and go on to better things. Keep walking. Don't stop.

Greaves did not stop. Marching into the heat haze – or, more accurately, dragging his feet behind him, through the heavy, burning sand – he kept himself going by dwelling on where he had come from and what the end of his bitter journey might bring him.

He recalled his elegant family home in Hanover Street, Edinburgh, his student days at the University, romance with his girlfriend, now fiancée, Mary Radnor; then recruit training and his first years with the Scots Guards; and, finally, his baptism of fire in Sicily with 8 Commando, leading to that unforgettable day when, outside Mersa Brega, the awesome might of Rommel's Afrika Korps – hundreds of tanks, thousands of men – had swept over the British defences and pushed them all the way back to Tobruk and the Mediterranean.

Whether a defeat or not, that last adventure had been the most exciting time of Greaves's life to date.

Disturbing though it was to acknowledge the fact, Greaves had enjoyed the experience, had taken pride from surviving it, and was still feeling proud when recuperating from his painful wounds in the hospital in Alexandria, where he had first met Captain David Stirling, likewise Scots Guards, who had led him to where he was this very moment.

That pride sustained him even now as, scorched by the sun, his throat dry, his head aching, his eyes bloodshot and practically blind, he continued to stumble on towards that dazzling horizon.

He would not stop. He had a lot to look forward to. He would drink a cooling beer, eat a decent meal, be flown out to Cairo and, if he was lucky, even be reunited with Nurse Frances Beamish in the relative luxury of Shepheard's Hotel. Life was for the living, he realized, and he wanted to live.

That romantic notion kept Greaves going when his exhausted body begged him to give in.

Nor did any of the others stop. Captains Stirling and Callaghan, Corporal Clayton, Privates Ashman, Privates Turner and Moffatt and all the others. Though hungry and thirsty, though burnt and blistered, though mentally and physically exhausted, they refused to give in. They hiked, marched, walked and, in some cases, eventually crawled, until they saw what some of them thought was a mirage: the palm trees, green grass and pale-blue water of Jalo Oasis.

Jimbo was on his hands and knees. Having collapsed, he had started crawling. After crawling on his belly for what seemed like an eternity, he had risen back onto his hands and knees. He was wearing shorts and his knees were blistered. The blisters burst and were scraped by sand. The raw flesh of Jimbo's knees poured blood that soaked the sand and the pain, which was beyond his imagining, made him shed silent tears.

His hands were blistered, too. The burning sand burst those blisters. When the pus poured out, the hot sand scorched his raw skin and made him almost cry out with the pain. Almost, but not quite. Jimbo gritted his teeth instead. He advanced on blistered hands and knees, in the agony of the damned, leaving a trail of blood behind him, towards what he was convinced was a mirage of cool water and shade.

'Won't give in,' he gasped. 'Never!'

Someone walked out towards him, stopped above him, looked down at him. He was a very big man in an immaculate uniform, his arms folded across his broad chest as he gazed down in wonder.

'You're a right bloody mess,' LRDG Sergeant

'Wild Bill' Monnery said with a widening grin. 'Welcome home, trooper.'

Jimbo smiled and collapsed.

18

The SAS raids of December 1941 had accounted for ninety-seven aircraft, according to L Detachment's meagre records. Also destroyed, however, were at least forty vehicles, including fuel tankers invaluable to the Axis forces.

In March, June and December of the following year, having learnt from their good and bad experiences, the SAS mounted a number of successful raids around Benghazi and Tobruk, destroying shipping and supply dumps as well as airfields.

When Rommel's Afrika Korps advanced into Egypt, L Detachment, SAS, by then equipped with its own jeeps armed with mounted Vickers and Browning machine-guns, destroyed many enemy aircraft with Lewes bombs and machine-gun fire in raids against the airfields of Bagoush and Sidi Haneish.

Whatever the precise number of Axis losses, General Auchinleck, the British Commander-in-Chief of Middle East Forces, was satisfied that L Detachment had indeed proved its worth. Captain Stirling was therefore promoted to Major and allowed to recruit a further six officers and up to forty other ranks.

The deeds of L Detachment, and of Captain Stirling, soon became legendary, particularly in the folklore of service bars throughout the Middle East.

In October 1942, L Detachment, now 500 strong, was officially listed as 1st Special Air Service (SAS) Regiment.

Though the creator and official head of the SAS, Captain Stirling did not stay with it for long, being captured by the Germans in January 1943, during Operation Torch in Tunisia, then incarcerated in Gavi prison, Italy, from where he escaped four times, before being sent to the high-security Colditz Prison, where he remained as a POW for the rest of the war.

The future of the SAS Regiment was, however, assured when, in 1943, Captain Stirling's brother, Lieutenant-Colonel William Stirling, then with the British First Army, formed 2 SAS and, with the Special Raiding Squadron (SRS) – which was 1

SAS temporarily renamed – performed invaluable work in the Allied capture of Sicily.

In October 1945 the SAS was officially disbanded because the War Office saw no future need for it. However, in 1947, the War Office, changing its tune, established a Territorial Army raiding unit attached to the Rifle Brigade, which was then merged with the Artists Rifles and renamed 21 SAS (Artists).

In 1950, during the so-called 'Emergency' in Malaya, Colonel 'Mad' Mike Calvert, veteran of the Chindit campaigns in Burma, formed the Malayan Scouts, which included a detachment from 21 SAS (Artists). In 1952, at the recommendation of Colonel Calvert, 22 SAS was created from the Malayan Scouts as a special counterinsurgency force.

Many of those who had fought with Stirling during World War Two rushed to join 22 SAS, serving with it during many remarkable campaigns in many parts of the world.

Within a decade, the SAS became the most famous regiment in the world. Whether reviled or admired, criticized or deified, it remains that way still.

OTHER BOOKS IN THIS SERIES

Available now at newsagents and booksellers

SOLDIER A SAS: Behind Iraqi
Lines   £4.99

SOLDIER B SAS: Heroes of the
South Atlantic   £4.99

SOLDIER C SAS: Secret War
in Arabia   £4.99

SOLDIER D SAS: The Colombian
Cocaine War   £4.99

SOLDIER E SAS: Sniper Fire
in Belfast   £4.99

SOLDIER F SAS: Guerrillas in
the Jungle   £4.99

SOLDIER H SAS: The Headhunters
of Borneo   £4.99